The Six-Lined Racerunner

What a lizard taught me about life, growing up, and finding my way

A Memoir

Steven L. Orebaugh

SUNBURY PRESS
Mechanicsburg, PA USA

Published by Sunbury Press, Inc.
Mechanicsburg, PA USA

SUNBURY
PRESS

www.sunburypress.com

For information about special discounts for bulk purchases, please contact Sunbury Press Orders Dept. at (855) 338-8359 or orders@sunburypress.com.

To request one of our authors for speaking engagements or book signings, please contact Sunbury Press Publicity Dept. at publicity@sunburypress.com.

FIRST SUNBURY PRESS EDITION: December 2025

Set in Adobe Garamond | Interior design by Crystal Devine | Cover by Darleen Sedjro | Edited by Sarah Peachey.

Publisher's Cataloging-in-Publication Data
Names: Orebaugh, Steven L., author.
Title: The six-lined racerunner : what a lizard taught me about life, growing up, and finding my way / Steven L. Orebaugh.
Description: First trade paperback edition. | Mechanicsburg, PA : Sunbury Press, 2025.
Summary: In his struggle to overcome an almost pathological shyness, a young military child is aided by the encouragement of his loving parents, two intrepid friends, and an impeccable fifth-grade teacher. The boys' love for catching and collecting lizards leads them into a variety of adventures as they search for the elusive six-lined racerunner.
Identifiers: ISBN : 979-8-88819-354-9 (softcover).
Subjects: BIOGRAPHY & AUTOBIOGRAPHY / Memoirs | FAMILY & RELATIONSHIPS / Military Families | YOUNG ADULT NONFICTION / General.

Designed in the USA
0 1 1 2 3 5 8 13 21 34 55

For the Love of Books!

This book is dedicated to military families who support our Soldiers, Sailors, Marines, and Airmen in their duties in the U.S. and the world over.

One

"Stop," I mouthed, frantically signaling to my friend, Mark Godwin, to stay where he was. Black-haired, dark-eyed, and slight, he was standing on the other side of a small collection of gnarled shrubs, just off the path I was standing on. I held my finger to my lips. It was a tense situation, one that called for stealth and delicacy. He froze in his tracks, brown eyes peering intently at me.

"Rat-tail," I said, as quietly as I could, and he nodded.

We were stalking a rat-tailed racerunner, a super-fast lizard with red markings on its side and tail longer than its body. We had manipulated it into position between us, but I was pretty sure the little animal was aware only of me. Mark's presence would be a surprise, and if I could flush it in that direction, I figured we could catch the speedy reptile if we handled things with care and precision.

I grinned and pointed. He was smaller than most of the ones we'd seen, but a beautiful specimen. The tiny head turned back toward me as though he was studying me, and I could just make out the fine, rhythmic motions of his chest as he caught his breath. The thin tail twitched back and forth as I moved deftly forward, careful to avoid snapping any twigs or crunching any brittle leaves that might spook him into running before we were ready to spring our trap.

"Now!" I cried, rushing toward the collection of dry leaves where the lizard had taken refuge.

In a fraction of a second, with astonishing speed, the reptile shot out in Mark's direction and, shockingly, found itself in the grasp of a highly satisfied sixth-grader.

"You got him!"

This was an unexpected turn of events. The rat-tails were very elusive, and we could probably only catch one out of every five we saw down in the gullies.

Mark held him up proudly, and I inspected him.

"Wow, that's great! Let's get him up with the other ones. Maybe we can get him something to make him feel more at home."

We were obsessed with creating a natural haven for the lizards we caught, certain they would thrive if we could duplicate their surroundings. We grabbed some sticks, and I found a stone just the right size for him to hide under.

"We must have caught ten—it's been a great day!"

Mark agreed, and we walked up the long grade toward my home, one of many housing units in the complex called "Los Encinares de Los Reyes," or Royal Oaks. All the housing units were long, rectangular, two-story affairs with flat roofs, each containing four apartments. They were made of either red brick or concrete painted white. Mark's dad and mine were both enlisted men in the U.S. Air Force, so they didn't rate housing on the actual base at Torrejon, which was reserved for officers.

The unit I lived in was on the upper story, perched at the top of a hill that overlooked an expansive slope of undeveloped land interlaced with deep, steep-sided ravines we called "the gullies." This small wilderness area was ringed by perhaps a dozen housing units. The gullies were dry-washes, typical of the arid topography in the undulating landscape of central Spain. These parched lands, when not cultivated, were covered by spindly, sticky sagebrush shrubs, along with a few stunted trees, offering the lizards some shelter from predators. Well-trodden paths meandered among the sage, intersecting here and there. If we looked out beyond these gullies from my porch, we could see some trees down in a valley that hid a small stream we called "the sewers" because the water smelled kind of funny. This creek, where we sometimes went to catch tadpoles, was right behind the school. Beyond, in the hazy distance, lay the outskirts of Madrid, a jumble of high-rises barely visible through the smog that continually enveloped the capital city.

The gullies were our favorite grounds for catching lizards. The ones we chased were mostly an everyday sort of earth-colored creature we called "brownies," but occasionally, we were fortunate enough to encounter a more exotic variety, like the rat-tailed racerunner we'd just captured.

"I'll let them go tonight. Guess what—we're going on vacation tomorrow!" I was elated as I delivered that bit of exciting news.

"Wow! Where're you going? And how long?"

"Down to Sevilla. We went there two years ago. There's a swimming pool right at the motel! And the Reimoldses are going with us!"

"You're going on vacation with TC?"

"Yep. And her mom and dad. And Kathy and Robbie, of course."

He suddenly looked a little sad. "We don't have a lot of lizard-catching time left."

Mark was right. The end of summer was coming up, and fast.

"It's OK. When I get back, we'll still have a few days left before school starts."

"We can catch some more. Maybe set a record!"

"Yeah," I agreed. "And we gotta go to the pool a couple more times."

Holding our prisoner carefully, Mark and I climbed the stairs to our porch, which the Spanish called a terazza. We placed the lizard carefully in the center of our bucket and proceeded to take inventory.

"Hey, that's eleven. Ten brownies and a rat-tail." I shook the bucket, trying to stir up some activity. "Nobody catches as many as we do," I bragged.

Mark was as proud of our achievements as I was. "Yeah, but still no six-line. Where do they hide?" he pondered wistfully.

We had long fantasized about finding and capturing the rarest and fastest of the lizards, the six-lined racerunner. These were legendary in our eyes. Few of the boys in Royal Oaks had even seen one, let alone caught one.

"Well," I stipulated, "we're gonna get one before we leave. How can we go back home again if we don't?"

I had thrown out this challenge numerous times before, and we were determined. The problem was, we could only catch them if we could find them. But obtaining a six-lined racerunner would give us a stature our peers would envy, of this we were confident. So, in the meantime, we just had to be content with capturing the lizards we found, trying to sharpen our skills.

I dreamt a lot about stature at that age. Like most boys, I wanted other kids to like me, but I was not someone who attracted attention. Catching that rare lizard would give us some bragging rights—it had become our sacred quest.

"We've got one more year," I said. "That's a long time. I'm sure we'll catch one by then."

It was the summer of 1971, and I had just turned ten. Both Mark's family and mine were approaching the end of our time in Spain, and pressure was building for us to make good on our quest to capture the six-lined racerunner.

Mark fell silent, studying me. "I can still see that scar on the side of your head."

I wore my hair pretty short, a "GI cut," like my dad's. And the scar was a big one. "My mom says it'll get smaller over time. You know, kinda heal up some more."

"That's OK. I think it's cool. Like Frankenstein."

We both laughed.

Really, I was pretty fortunate, given what I'd been through. The summer before, in a bizarre accident during a game of hide-and-seek with friends, a collision with another boy had left me with a depressed skull fracture and a concussion. The Air Force hospital at Torrejon, where my dad worked in the administrative office, was relatively small. There was no neurosurgeon there, so I was flown to an Air Force base in Germany for an evaluation.

My mom and dad flew with me on a big Red Cross plane. I had only been on an airplane once before, on the flight to Spain, so I was pretty nervous, but my father talked me through the takeoff. It was a big propeller plane, which flew a lot lower than the jets. We could see the roads and towns far below us as though we had been suspended above a miniature landscape, which fascinated me. At one point, Dad looked at me curiously and shook his head, patting me on the shoulder.

"Steve, you're the only boy I know who could get a life-threatening head injury from playing hide-and-seek."

I just shrugged, clutching my favorite matchbox car, a Lamborghini Miura, which I'd taken with me for good luck in the hospital. My suggestion of a small terrarium with a few lizards for the windowsill in my hospital room was quickly rejected.

Honestly, I wasn't sure how the accident had happened. Brian Hilliard and I had both run as fast as we could to the clothesline pole, which was the home base, from opposite ends of the yard. Anticipating the collision, we both dodged in the same direction, and his chin collided with the side of my head. When I came to, I was lying on the ground, dazed. I remembered seeing big yellow stars that quickly faded away.

Just a few weeks later, when the dent in my head was much more apparent, we checked into the vast military hospital in Wiesbaden, Germany, and within two days I had to undergo brain surgery. At least they told me it was brain surgery, but it was mostly just to fix my broken skull and get some old blood out. The boy in the bed next to me, Herman, had a brain tumor, and after his operation he couldn't talk quite right. I spent a lot of nights up there thinking about him. The evening before I left, we ate strawberry ice cream together, and we both threw up in the hallway the next morning. When I boarded the plane to fly home, I was wearing a big bandage on my head that looked like a turban. That's how I started fourth grade.

But everything went back to normal after that, and I soon did all the usual things, including catching lizards, my favorite pastime. I was a shy boy, given to prowling the gullies by myself or with Mark. I melted away in crowds and was reluctant to compete, last to speak up, and first to give way. The head injury only made this worse. Moving from place to place every couple of years probably contributed as well; Royal Oaks was the fifth place I'd lived by the time I was seven years old. My father noted these disturbing traits in me at a very young age, and he unceasingly encouraged me to break out of my introversion.

Dad loved baseball and ensured I went out for Little League each spring. In his eyes, the camaraderie, the teamwork, and the acquisition of athletic skills were just what I needed. Truthfully, I was more content to search for our tiny reptilian quarry, read comic books, or play with electric trains in my room. I wasn't confident in myself in crowds, and I was fearful of competition.

Mark squinted in the bright sunlight as we proudly examined our bucket terrarium. He was my best lizard-catching buddy, a tried-and-true comrade for over a year. Life had been lonely for me during the first years in Spain, but I finally met some other boys with similar interests, and we formed a little lizard-catching band. Over time, as the others moved away, I came to especially like Mark. He was as self-effacing as I was.

Sometimes, when we patrolled the sandy terrain, he and I traded stories about life before we came over to Torrejon, the days with our grandparents, aunts, uncles, and cousins back in the States. Mark had spent time in Montana with his father's side of the family and in New Hampshire with his mother's.

"Do they have lizards in Montana?" I somehow thought of it as a cowboy place, with open vistas, tall red rocks, and cactuses. I'd seen a western once, with the cowpokes driving vast herds of cattle up the country's center toward that fabled territory. On the way they'd had to cope with thirst, Indians, and rattlesnakes.

"I don't think so. I never saw one, anyway. It gets pretty cold, and they get lots of snow. It's not like it is here. They have some snakes, though."

"I don't get that. If snakes can live there, why not lizards?"

Neither of us had an answer to that quandary.

We had a special sort of bond, we Air Force families, dependent upon one another in an exotic, faraway place. But as much fun as living in Torrejon could be, we all dreamed of being back home, in our own country, surrounded by familiar things. And it made us happy, if a little homesick, to talk about the people, the cities, and the countryside we'd left behind.

Being pulled away from the comfortable cocoon of stateside life, whether in a friendly little town, on an Air Force base, or in a peaceful neighborhood on the edge of a city, gave us all a chance to grow in directions we otherwise wouldn't have. We just didn't know it then.

Two

"When we get back from vacation," my dad said as I struggled to open my eyes, "we can go down and get some batting practice. Nobody is on those diamonds now."

I had just awakened from a long nap in the back seat of our Peugeot as we traveled southward on the Autopista, a Spanish highway, into Andalucia. The prospect of going on vacation was thrilling, especially since our friends, the Reimoldses, were coming with us. They were one of several families that became close friends of ours when we were overseas, and we have remembered them fondly ever after. The Air Force, in its wisdom, had stitched a tightly woven web of support around us, and for that, we were most grateful. The people made the peripatetic lifestyle and the lack of continuity bearable.

Stretching and blinking in the bright sunlight, I thought about the baseball season, which had ended a few weeks prior. It seemed like an awfully long time until I would have to face spring tryouts. I didn't want anxieties about baseball to encumber me while on vacation, so I was eager to change the subject.

"Look, Dad!" I said excitedly, leaning forward.

"Well, I'm glad you're finally awake. I trust you had a nice nap."

I brushed off his gentle sarcasm. "No, look—Veterano Osborne!"

Our Peugeot sped up a long rise, colorful poppies and fields of golden grain streaming by us. I looked out the windshield to see a dark figure perched at the top of the hill, the massive silhouette of a bull, head erect as if surveying the valley below him. These towering billboards were not unusual sights along the main roads in the southern part of the country—they were merely advertisements for a local brand of sherry—but to me, they were both beckoning and foreboding. I placed great importance on the enormous black signs, which, in my young mind, represented an enigmatic symbol of Spain and its people.

I glanced over at my sister, who remained in peaceful slumber, curled into her corner of the back seat.

Dad still wanted to talk about my performance on the baseball diamond. "Steve, I think you need to step into the ball more. You have a level swing, but you pull your foot out of the box. You have to stay in there and put the bat on the ball. Remember in Cumberland how you used to hit the ball over the house when Grandaddy was pitching?"

He was right, but Grandaddy had been tossing a Wiffle ball. The hardball in Little League was a different story—too often, the ball looked like it was coming right at me. Even though I had only been hit by a pitch once, I wasn't keen on having that happen again. I just couldn't stay close to the plate when the pitcher fired the baseball toward me.

"And we'll do some pop-ups. You need to come charging at the ball. You know, be aggressive."

I don't know exactly how my behavior on the ball field would have been described, but I'm sure no one would have called it "aggressive."

"That's how you become a good fielder. Like Roberto Clemento." I could sense my father smiling as he drove this point home. Even though I couldn't pronounce the player's name, I was a big fan of Roberto Clemente, the outstanding Pirate outfielder. Dad got a kick out of saying it just the way I did.

"Jerry, he has to be careful. He's only a year out from the operation," my mother interjected.

My reluctance on the baseball field had only intensified after I'd suffered the head injury a year before.

My sister had now awakened and was looking curiously through the back window. "Are they back there?" she asked, yawning and stretching.

I could see our friends not far behind us. They drove an enormous 1968 maroon-and-white Oldsmobile that took up more than half of the narrow highway. It was as much a boat as a car, an object of adoration in every Spanish town into which Mr. Reimolds could maneuver it. Their family had two daughters the same ages as my sister and me, and they were coming to Sevilla with us, which made the prospect of the holiday much more exciting.

Kathy waved furiously at the car, and I could just make out Mrs. Reimolds waving in return from her perch, close beside her husband on the big bench seat in front.

At that moment, we pulled off the highway into a small town in search of lunch. The village before us consisted of a mass of stone dwellings, none higher than two stories, which lined impossibly narrow streets, most leading to a central square, where a fountain served as a gathering point. The stone walls of many of the houses were simply stacked—I couldn't see any mortar between them. Some of the walls leaned precariously, and all the buildings were roofed with terra-cotta tile, as was typical in Spain. There was a quaintness about the town, which must have existed solely to support the local farmers, for there was no evidence of a factory or any industry.

The Peugeot negotiated the tiny streets easily enough, but the Olds was another issue. I looked back to see the expansive car lumbering dangerously close to walls and curbs. Somehow, Mr. Reimolds guided it through.

"Quite a spectacle," my father said, grinning and glancing at the rearview mirror.

As we got out, the townspeople observed us quietly. Swarthy, dark-haired, and dark-eyed, they watched with expectation and suspicion as we collected on the narrow sidewalk. I hated being the center of attention among people who wondered why a group of strangers had suddenly appeared in their town. Still, there was little to do except make our way toward one of the small cafes that ringed the plaza.

During the three years we'd spent in Spain, we'd been to many villages around Madrid, sightseeing or visiting small factories or workshops where we could purchase handmade goods for very little money. The people lived threadbare lives, just as their ancestors had, and they were tied to the land and the towns by invisible forces of culture and tradition that I could not perceive. The older men wore tweed or herringbone jackets and berets with dark pants, while their elderly wives always seemed to be in dark gray or black skirts or dresses. Their faces were creased with decades of life's stresses, and their glances seemed dark and suspicious. The young people, however, were less inclined to regard us as pernicious and would look us in the eye. The girls were quite affable, and frequently walked arm in arm, displaying a physical affection that was alien to us. The boys were bold and handsome, with flashing eyes and a great attraction to blond women, including my sister. At fourteen, she was tall and shapely, with long, straight yellow hair that was a magnet for the Spaniards. If a car attracted their initial attention, the presence of a *chica rubia* brought the boys of the pueblo to a standstill.

"How about this one, Dad?" I asked as we crossed the plaza.

"Any bodega will do, as long as we can get some food!" he grumbled. The men in my family get a little testy when their blood sugars get low.

The front door of the bar was ajar on this warm morning, and in its place were chains of plastic beads that one pushed aside to enter. My father once told me that such chains were there to "keep the flies out," but they weren't very effective. Inside, the place was dark and fragrant with the smells of typical Spanish cuisine: grilled lamb, shrimp, garlic, eggs, onions, olive oil. It also smelled, in a comforting way, of the people who lived there and frequented this small bar.

A small group of older men, *viejos*, outfitted in shabby jackets and engrossed in animated conversation, regarded us as we entered, their throaty chatter falling to silence almost immediately. We were not only intruders but *extranjeros*, people from another culture. The bar was greasy, the chairs wooden and functional, and the large mirror behind the many dark bottles on the shelves behind the bar was pretty messy. It was a typical Spanish tavern.

"Hola, señor," my father offered uncertainly to a grizzled and officious bartender who appeared startled at our entrance.

11

Reluctantly, the man waved to some barstools, and we placed ourselves upon them, self-conscious but hungry.

"Bocadillos? Jamon?" I asked, looking longingly at a beautiful Serrano ham hanging behind the bar.

My father beamed. My Spanish was, at best, elementary, but I far exceeded my parents' linguistic capabilities. Speaking Spanish in front of my family gave me a sense of pride. Though I was usually shy amid strangers, this was my moment to step into the limelight and make our needs known.

The squat, unshaven man behind the counter melted, smiling at me under his bushy gray mustache. The old men at the table turned back to their conversation, the din of the bar returned, and the room suddenly felt inviting. The bartender placed a small bowl of olives in front of us, a delectable, local treat. The Spanish people could be cold, aloof, and apathetic when approached by foreigners—and they frequently reacted that way to the GIs who wandered off the bases and into the local communities. We had learned that the hard way. But if you were willing to spend time to learn a bit of the language, no matter how badly you stumbled or how terrible your pronunciation, your attempt evoked a completely different response. Stilted Castilian Spanish could dispel the icy intolerance we were accorded at first glance.

TC, the Reimolds' younger daughter, put her elbows on the bar, rested her chin on her hands, and looked around. Perched on a stool beside me, she let her legs dangle aimlessly, kicking them gently back and forth. She seemed happy all the time, and it was easy to be around her—even though she was a girl.

In a few minutes, the man behind the bar spread plates of ham on crusty bread in front of us, which we gulped down with the salty olives and small bottles of orange Fanta or Coca-Cola. After our disruptive arrival, things had returned to normal in the pueblo.

"We should go take a look in their church," I heard my mother saying to Mrs. Reimolds. "In every little town, there's a parish church, and each one has relics from the patron saints that are hundreds of years old. Usually, there's a fortune's worth of gold and silver chalices, goblets, crucifixes . . . it's the hidden wealth of the Catholic Church."

My sister shot a glance at her friend, Robbie, and both of them rolled their eyes at the prospect of spending an hour looking at antiques in an ancient church.

Mom could look at ancient artifacts all day, especially if they were religious. Her life had been intertwined with the Roman Catholic Church since her arrival on earth, and its history fascinated her. She had received all the normal sacraments, faithfully reported for Mass each week, and attended diocesan schools in Pittsburgh for her entire education. Amid those years, she spent some months in a Catholic orphanage with her siblings when my grandmother experienced what was then termed a "nervous breakdown" in the wake of my grandfather abandoning her and the young family. He had left her penniless, with no skills, no employment, a tubal pregnancy, and four hungry children. Eventually, Grandma became a cook at the Stouffer's restaurant downtown and was able to remove her children from the orphanage, caring for them as a single mother of meager means. My mother had a healthy appreciation of the Church, given all it had done for her, but also a realistic, and, perhaps at times even cynical, understanding of the imperfections that laced its complicated structure and its all-too-fallible servants.

But we were running behind schedule, and my father gently dismissed the idea of a foray into the town's church. Back out on the street again, we looked back to find a trail of interested young men following Kathy and Robbie at a respectful distance.

"See you in Sevilla!" I called to the Reimoldses as they got into their car.

From the first moment I met her, Mrs. Reimolds had been an ardent supporter of mine. It was no secret in either of our families that I was a timid little boy. Lacking even the most elemental sense of confidence, I was hesitant to approach a cashier or to ask someone for directions to the bathroom in the classroom. I stayed quiet, hoping to attract as little attention from my teachers as possible. My father's exhortations and my mother's supportive suggestions failed to change my demeanor. But the kindness and attention Mrs. Reimolds offered me at our every meeting instilled in me a germ of self-regard. No one cheered louder at my baseball games, greeted me quite as enthusiastically at their front door, or sang "Happy Birthday" to me with more vigor.

Within a few minutes of our arrival at the motel, my sister and I put on our swimsuits and tiptoed out onto a searing hot sidewalk, headed for the swimming pool. Kathy smelled like summer to me as I hurried behind her, the distinct essence of suntan lotion wafting off her skin. The pool was deserted, and we plunged in, laughing and holding our noses. TC and Robbie soon made their way out as well, and while our older sisters sunned and preened, TC and I dove for quarters we'd thrown into the water, compared handstands, and played Marco Polo. The pool was shallow, except at one end, and, surrounded by the wings of the motel, it made for a splendid playground on the outskirts of the historic city. Baked by a sun perched high in a cloudless sky, we had arrived in paradise. Any other activities on this vacation would clearly be secondary.

In the evening, we dressed and went to dinner, finding a café with outdoor tables on the Guadalquivir River. My mother, the family historian, explained that the storied waterway had once served as a route to transport the riches of the New World to the interior of the country, ruled by the Catholic monarchs of Spain, Ferdinand and Isabella. And it was upon this river that many of the great Spanish explorers had begun their bold journeys to the West, ushering in a new age of exploration, discovery, conquest, and colonization.

"Isn't it hard to believe that so many things happened right here on this very river?" she prodded me. "The very first voyage around the world, guided by Ferdinand Magellan, began in Sevilla!"

"Sangria, por favor," my father said to the waiter, who graciously approached the table in a flash of Spanish bravado, calling out to busboys to bring us *agua fria* while laying out the silverware and doting romantically over the ladies.

In a few moments, the parents were toasting liberally and enjoying great conviviality, courtesy of Spanish red wine mixed with fruit, buoyed by the warm effervescence that friendship and spirits provide. As children, we were transfixed by this transformation, embracing the joy our parents were clearly experiencing.

A handsome Spanish busboy with slicked-back dark hair had caught sight of Kathy and Robbie. I noticed him perpetually refilling our water glasses, hovering watchfully around our table. A mere sip from a glass, and he was back, nodding and refilling.

Sevilla was even more *encantando*—enchanting—by night than it was by day. Sitting by the languid river, we had a stimulating view of the downtown and historical area, and across the water stood a landmark, a stone tower called the Torre del Oro, or tower of gold, which dated from the times when the Moors controlled southern Spain. On this night, the historic structure was bathed in a soft amber glow, majestically reflected in the river. A yellow moon hung low over the city. The evening had the peculiar character of a moment you remember forever after—not just in your thoughts but in a profound feeling that embeds itself deep within.

"Steven, what have you been doing lately? Are you building any models? Or spending most of your summer outside?"

Mrs. Reimolds had a way of drawing me into the conversation, endorsing whatever I was into at the time, and making me forget my shyness. I told her about the plastic airplane I was assembling, proud to have my interests showcased for the moment.

"And catching lizards—me and Mark caught twenty-one last week!"

She seemed impressed, but my dad frowned. He had warned me about keeping too many of the little reptiles in too close quarters. After a frank conversation, he'd convinced me of the importance of "catch and release."

The following day, we made our way to our cars for a trip to the historic district. The sun was already bright and warm, and I looked longingly at the crystal-clear water in the pool as we strolled by. A few bathers had already begun the bronzing process.

The people of Sevilla were different in character than the Madrilenos I had come to know: darker in color, more joyous, intent upon fairs and festivals, emerging at night to clap, sing, and dance in breathtaking, flashy costumes to the rhythm of classical guitar. The sultry weather itself instilled a sense of felicity and promised a different life altogether in this wondrous place.

The streets of Sevilla were already alive at this early hour with indescribable energy, a festival atmosphere that seemed inherent in this city. It wasn't so in Madrid, imbued as it was with a sense of self-importance. Clerks and ministers in suits scurried down the wide boulevards, lined with massive government buildings—some ornate, some drab and square. But everywhere in Sevilla, there was a riot of color. Bright cascades of flowers toppled off spindly wrought iron on every whitewashed dwelling or storefront, and the gardens teemed with colorful blooms. Women wore colorful dresses and decorated their tresses with exotic blossoms.

After we parked, TC and I ran across the street to the cathedral. Enormous and foreboding, the Gothic structure soared toward the heavens with myriad arches and buttresses, accented on one corner by an even taller, more imposing square tower that presided over the entire city with a somber gravity. This tower, the Giralda, was originally built to provide self-defense for the city. It contained a long series of sloping ramps that gently rose to a captivating overlook from an enclosed observation platform at the top.

TC was a whole lot more fun to tour with than I'd imagined a girl could be. I'm sure she would rather have been looking at flamenco dolls or dress patterns, but she was content to go with me to the places I wanted to see. She showed as much enthusiasm as I did for the historical implements on display, including a host of suits of armor and the weapons soldiers wielded in the Middle Ages.

Off we scrambled, ascending the ramps through the gloomy stone halls as fast as we could. As we climbed, I fancied that I could hear the clatter of armor around the next corner, imagining I would encounter a knight on his steed, peering at me through the nefarious slits in his metallic headpiece, shouting at us to move aside as he galloped by. Finally, we reached the top, a large, drafty chamber that faced broad vistas on each of the four sides, looking out over the bustling city and the countryside beyond.

For a few minutes, on top of the Giralda tower, it was just TC and me, looking over all of Sevilla, and I felt a warm kinship with her. The world was small and far away, and I had a friend with me. I watched a man far below, helping his wife or girlfriend out of their car. It put me in mind of the times we'd spent in TC's room, playing with Barbie and Ken, and the sports car that Ken drove when he came to visit her. I would never tell my friends that I was playing with dolls, but it seemed natural with TC. I had my own Major Matt Mason dolls, but we considered those action figures, so they got a pass. At any rate, I always had fun when I went to TC's house, and spending time with her on vacation was pretty neat.

Our families arrived, breaking the spell, as they chatted happily about Spain and its culture. Except for Kathy and Robbie, who sullenly brought up the rear.

"Race ya down," I called merrily to TC.

And the two of us were off, running back to the base of the Giralda and into the cool darkness of the brooding cathedral. Almost inconceivably large, the structure somehow dovetailed with a small boy's impression of God. The soaring, symmetric arches within thrust toward the heavens; the tall stained-glass windows refracted the sunlight into hundreds of tiny, colorful points that moved slowly across the cold stone floors like migrating rainbows.

Moving reverently through the colossal structure, we spoke in hushed tones. The largest Gothic cathedral in the world had a grandiosity about it, a fantastic aura of historical importance. We moved slowly from one chapel to the next, small alcoves tucked in along the sides of the massive walls; each had some special significance. There was a plethora of gold—gold chalices, gold crucifixes, and intricate gold patterns in the lattice that adorned the cold gray walls above the altars.

A quiet Mass was in progress in one of the smaller side chapels. We tiptoed past as the penitent whispered their devotions.

"And Christopher Columbus is buried here?" Mr. Reimolds, a man of few words, seemed impressed.

"He is. See that sarcophagus?"

We strained our eyes as my mother pointed to a casket in the distance, held aloft by four figures bearing the eternal weight of the man who had introduced Western Europe to the New World.

"Hey, look, TC!" I dashed up to the velvet ropes surrounding the funereal scene. "See those flags? They belonged to the *Nina*, the *Pinta*, and the *Santa Maria*!"

We had learned all about Columbus's voyage in our Spanish classes, down to the last detail.

"Honestly? The real flags?" Her eyes were alight.

"That's what they say." I nodded confidently. We'd taken a tour with a docent during a visit two years earlier.

Ever the skeptic, my sister had to add her opinion. "They say he's buried in like five places all over Spain. Who knows if it's the real one?"

I didn't yet have a great understanding of cynicism or sarcasm, but Kathy seemed to have mastered both.

"Mom, can we get a corte?" I asked excitedly, as we emerged into the heat of the afternoon.

A corte was a cut of Neapolitan ice cream, between two crisp wafers. They sold them on street corners everywhere I'd ever been in Spain, and they were delicious. We had been warned by the public health people on base not to eat the Spanish dairy products, as they didn't reliably pasteurize the milk, but sometimes the allure was just too great. My mother gave me a few pesetas, and TC and I bounded to the corner to get in line at the stand.

We found a spot of shade in a small garden nearby and sat down to eat. It was now early afternoon, and the heat was nearly unbearable, at least for the grownups.

A lazy lizard sprawled on the pavement, watching us from nearby. TC noted my gaze and probably read my mind. "Maybe we'll see some by the pool—we're going back soon."

Turning to my father, I asked if I might be allowed to get a small figurine from the cathedral's gift store. I had a small army of hand-painted knights at home, one from each of the many historical towns or fortresses we'd visited.

My parents were tolerant of my whims. With a hundred-peseta note in my fist, I raced off with TC to the gift shop to see what military forces were marshaled there.

I bought a foot soldier with a huge broadsword and, to fight him off, a knight on horseback with a large shield and a battle axe. He looked prepared for pretty much anything, and so did his horse.

We spent the remainder of the afternoon back at the pool, diving, jumping, and competing while holding our breath under water. TC and I liked to see who could do the most flips and backflips without coming up for air.

A small collection of boys had coalesced near our sisters, who lay oblivious to their attentions in the harsh rays of the sun.

"What are they looking at?" I asked TC, surprised the two girls attracted such a crowd.

She grimaced. "I don't know. It's just Robbie."

I looked at her face in the bright sunlight. TC had more freckles than any girl I knew, which was funny because neither her mother nor her father looked very freckly to me. My mom said she was "as cute as a bug's ear," which left me wondering what that meant. I'd done my share of bug collecting—not too many of them were cute. And you couldn't really see their ears.

"Are you looking forward to starting school again?" she asked, helping the injured knight off the field of battle while I guided the other one in a march of victory.

I looked at her, startled. "No, not really. I'd rather just play. School gets so boring."

"I know," she offered, then added, thoughtfully, "but it's still fun to see all your friends and get to know your teacher. And meet new friends."

At that point in my life, I was beginning to comprehend how women formed the essential backbone of our society, and learning to appreciate their fundamental cultural role as the defenders of time-honored traditions, morals, and family structure. While these attributes in the broader population were not yet visible to me, I saw them quite clearly in the women and girls around me: in the lessons my mother taught my sister, in TC's insistence on helping the wounded knight while we played with toy soldiers, and in her mother's kindness to just about everyone.

TC's optimistic outlook brought me back to my senses. Of course I had to return to school, and I would likely enjoy meeting new friends and my new teacher. It was intimidating to me, though—I wasn't exactly the most popular boy, and I keenly felt my stature in a room full of people I did not yet know.

Our week in Sevilla passed quickly, but we made time for trips to the beach at Cadiz and the U.S. Navy base at Rota, as well as a long-anticipated visit to Cordoba, where the world-famous mosque proved to be as astonishing as the photos we'd seen. The rows of arches in the bright interior appeared nearly infinite, perhaps the Muslim vision of heaven.

The final morning found us on the road early. I looked longingly at the pool as we crept by in the cool darkness.

"Steven, did you have a good time?" Mrs. Reimolds asked, guiding her girls toward the waiting car.

I nodded. It had been a splendid vacation, and having TC along to share the adventures made it all the better. I waved at her and jumped into the back of the Peugeot, drowsy and ready for a long nap as we drove northward to Madrid. I couldn't wait to get back to see Mark so we could do as many fun things as possible before the summer ended.

But I knew time was no longer on our side.

Three

"Go that way—quick!" I yelled at Mark.

Sometimes lizard-hunting called for subtlety, and other times for flat-out speed.

Dutifully, he circled to the other side of the bush, peering intently into the foliage. "Your way," Mark suddenly called, announcing he'd flushed the little lizard—one that we called a "brownie"—back in my direction.

I crouched, motionless, waiting for it to scamper from the bed of dry, crackly leaves that underlay the sage bushes.

It was nearly upon me, scampering at full speed out from the protective leaves of the bush, oblivious to the giant squatting directly over its escape route . . . and I had it! Mark and I had learned to remain completely stock-still and then, in an instant, abruptly dart out a hand and grasp the little creatures without harming them, a bit like the bill of a patient, predatory bird. At the beginning of our adventures, there were many miscues—especially broken tails. Grasping for the lizard a bit too slowly, we'd curl our fingers around its wiggling tail rather than its lithe body, while the lizard itself shot by and made its way back to a hole or a local hiding place. Evolution made for tails that would break off in a snake's mouth or a bird's beak, allowing the escapee to live another day, albeit with an ugly, stubby black bud of a replacement that really diminished their appeal—at least to those of us who admired their physical appearance. These black-tailed veterans prowled the gullies, some of them victims of our misadventures, while many others had escaped from hungry, frustrated predators.

Lizards never ceased to fascinate me, which may have been hard to understand for anyone not enthralled by their subtle charms. The lizards were quite similar and, within a given variety, their markings were only subtly different. Their reactions to capture varied, from the cowardly to the indifferent (but never aggressive), and their size showed some range. The small ones we caught most often were an unembellished group, with only the occasional fleck of color. These we called brownies, for their earth-brown tones that provided good camouflage. Still, we admired their reptilian features—the tiny darting black eyes, a comparatively long and skinny body, short and amazingly swift legs, a slender and mysteriously detachable tail. We reveled in their lizard-ness, without a better explanation for the fascination they held for us.

We also admired them as adversaries. They were challenging to catch, even for the experienced boy. After two years of learning their habits, we still collected only about a third or, on a good day, half of the brownies we flushed out. And that made the game most enjoyable—it was us versus them, and mostly they won. Like a fly fisherman with a stringer full of rainbow trout, we beamed with pride at the end of the day if we had five or six prized specimens to show for our efforts.

Royal Oaks was lined with retaining walls along the roads and driveways, made of light gray, granite-like stone. The mortar of these walls was prone to decay and developed cavities; some pretty big lizards inhabited the resulting chinks and holes. We referred to these guys as "greenies" with a note of respect. We seldom had a chance to do anything but observe these lunkers if one of them left its lair to adopt a sunny perch amid the stones. These lizards were big enough to give us pause, so we didn't try too hard to catch them.

Moments after I grasped the wiggling brownie, Mark came running around the bush, as breathless with excitement as I had been. I proudly held up the terrified creature so he and I could admire it. This one was on the timid side, now hanging limply between my fingers, looking sullenly at its captors, doubtless wondering when it would be eaten.

"That's great," Mark said triumphantly. "Five today. Where do you wanna keep them?"

That was always a bit of a debate—my house or Mark's? None of Mark's four sisters had much use for lizards, and I only had one sister to contend with, so, more often than not, they ended up at my place. My mom and dad were OK with captive lizards as long as I kept them out on the porch. But my father drew the line at snakes.

"Those," he noted firmly, "stay down in the gullies."

I never forgot his warning, though I once pointed out that the glass lizard had no legs and therefore looked exactly like a snake. He wasn't amused. Honestly, it wasn't an issue—we just didn't see many snakes. But lizards were everywhere. You could usually hear them scamper through the leaves before you saw them. Snakes, I imagined, slithered silently on through, unbeknownst to us.

"Well," I proposed, thinking about the possibilities, "let's take them to my house. I think we have some hamburger we can feed them. My mom won't care—they don't eat too much."

The real problem was that they wouldn't eat. At all. We enticed them with dead flies, hamburger meat, and little crickets, all to no avail. Once captured, their spirits seemed to sag. We labored to make their surroundings as much like their own homes as possible, but being stashed in the bottom of a yellow plastic pail, even with the hodge-podge of sticks, rocks, and sand we put into it, clearly left them depressed and apathetic. All the activities of a healthy life that we figured a lizard might cherish—eating, running, hiding, socializing with other brownies—were interrupted inside this prison. And this was the major obstacle to good lizard stewardship we had yet to overcome.

So despite our prowess as lizard hunters—*aficionados*, as the Spaniards might say—we were not successful lizard owners. After a few days of watching the poor animals stare, motionless, at the sides of the bucket, ignoring food and their fellow captives, sympathy and pity compelled us to release them. We would take them back to the gullies and reluctantly dump them onto the sandy earth near a bush so they could quickly find shelter. But even as we restored their liberty, they simply lay motionless, as if unable to comprehend they had been returned to their wild dominion. Standing beside them for several minutes until they got it, we remained close by to ward off any birds or other predators until their instincts revitalized and they scampered off into the vegetation.

"Maybe we could do a better job on the buckets," Mark suggested, peering proudly down at the sullen lizards, which had spread out in the bottom of the pail, avoiding each other as best they could.

I was baffled by their complete lack of activity or interest. Our endless striving to make the plastic cage a desirable habitat had yielded little success.

"Yeah. Maybe more places to hide?" I asked, shaking my head.

We scooped up sand and small stones, placing them into the bottom of the container, avoiding the lizards and piling things up between them.

Lugging the bucket up the stairs and onto my terraza, we placed it on the floor, just inside the shadow from the ill-fitting roof, so the lizards would get a mix of sunlight and shade as the sun moved across the sky. Mark looked out over the gullies, at the other housing units below us, and beyond, to where the school buildings were hidden in a small valley.

"It's the last day of summer. Maybe we should go to the pool while they get adjusted?" he said with his characteristic smile, squinting at me in the bright sunlight.

Mark was always grinning. When I first met him, he was in fourth grade and I was in third. He was on an opposing Little League baseball team, and I was in the outfield when he came up to bat. I heard the center fielder announce that "Smiley" was coming to the plate. Even when he struck out, Mark smiled, marching dutifully back to the dugout. I liked that about him. My friend had thin, glossy black hair (that I swear his mother cut under a bowl) and equally dark eyes that flashed with enthusiasm and, occasionally, with mischief.

While I thought about his suggestion of going to the pool, I glanced over the railing. Sometimes, when I looked down over the sloping terrain to the road that disappeared toward the school, I thought about my first day living in Royal Oaks. I'd taken the bus to school from the Hotel Balboa in Madrid, our third temporary residence in the city, and by far the least desirable. My mother was waiting for the movers at our new housing unit. My father was at work at the base hospital, about twenty miles from our housing complex. All the kids living in Royal Oaks walked to school until they were old enough to go to middle school on the base, but there were buses for those living out in Madrid. Dad instructed me to walk the short distance from school at the end of the day to a new home I'd never seen before. But the dwellings in Royal Oaks all looked alike. They were two-story rectangular structures made of either red brick or white stucco. The thought of distinguishing my new home from so many others that looked the same filled me with uncertainty, and my heart sank when the bell rang. I was filled with anxiety as I set out to follow my father's directions: "Leave the school, take the road at the top of the hill off to the right, and keep following it. Eventually, in about a mile, you'll see the little sign right next to the driveway, for 202. Then just walk along the driveway, up the stairs to 202C, and you'll be home!"

It hadn't exactly worked out that way. I took a wrong turn somewhere and ended up on a different road entirely. Dad eventually came home from work and drove out to find me. After weeks of commuting from Madrid, he was excited to finally have our family in the new home, but I sulked the whole way back to our new place.

When I stood on my terraza that warm afternoon with my friend and our bucket of lizards, peering at the twisting road below us, I thought about myself as a frightened, hesitant boy, walking to an unfamiliar dwelling with a bookbag and a Batman lunchbox, lonely and unsure of which way to go. Taller now, with two seasons of baseball and a brain surgery under my belt, I was ready to begin the fifth grade. I felt as though I'd made some progress since that unhappy day.

"Hey, before we go," Mark said, "let's play parachute man."

We put the lizards down for the moment, our attention drawn to an assortment of little plastic men with colorful plastic parachutes attached to their backs. We'd purchased them for five pesetas each at a little store on the other end of our housing complex that we referred to as the *fruteria*, a sort of mini-mart run by an old Spanish man with a perpetual scowl and a big gray mustache. The shop had fresh fruit and sundries, including a few distractions for kids behind the counter.

Mark ran down the stairs, shielding his eyes against the bright sunlight, and called up to me.

"OK, let 'em go!"

The terraza offered a good platform for launching airborne assaults since it was not only high off the ground, but the ground below it sloped steeply down to Mark's driveway. The game was to let fly with a whole company of airborne troops while the boy below ran around as fast as he could, trying to pull them out of the air before they hit the ground. You had the best chance of winning the assault if you slung them as far down the hill as possible. If the parachute didn't open, that one didn't count. Technically, we considered it an ineffective paratrooper.

I wadded up the parachute for the first man and then threw him as hard as I could, followed by another and another, and finally, a fourth. The gentle breeze caught the men's chutes and took them, aloft, down the hill while Mark ran wildly to catch them.

"One . . . Two . . . Three . . . aaagh!" He rushed down the steep embankment for the final one, nearly falling as the parachutist barely evaded his reach and floated to the ground.

"Well, that's three. My turn," I yelled.

He came panting up the steps, and we played the game in reverse, only I missed two of his.

"I think you might have thrown some of those guys out-of-bounds," I sulked, crestfallen, because I usually won.

"Nah. You were slow. That's all."

"Get your stuff," I called, rushing back up the steps as he rushed down.

26

I threw the airborne troops back onto the tile floor of the terraza and rushed in the front door to grab my towel and put on my swim trunks.

"Mom, we're going to the pool," I announced as I threw the door open.

"I thought you guys were getting your last lizards in before school," she called out from the kitchen. "Mr. Mazza is stopping by soon—I want you to say hi."

I stopped and cocked my head. "Who's Mr. Mazza?"

"I'm down here, Gerry," I heard someone call from the carport below us. The voice was not familiar to me, but it had a friendly ring.

"Come downstairs, Steve. I want you to meet our new neighbor," Mom called.

I ran down the concrete steps behind my mom and told Mark to come back up to my house. Getting new neighbors was always a thrill, and in Royal Oaks, people were constantly moving in and out. Most families were there for a three-year tour, but some were only there for a year or two. We became used to saying "goodbye" and "welcome" quite often. We'd recently bade farewell to the Reagans, a family from Texas, who had lived underneath us for the first couple of years we were at 202C. They were neighborly, but their children were much older than Kathy and me, so we never really bonded with them other than to call out "hello" now and then. Still, it was sad to see them go, and all of us left behind felt a pang of sadness and a bit of envy at the sight of a family packing up and heading back to the States.

There is, at times, a sense of estrangement for military families living overseas. To be sure, there were elements of stateside culture that regularly made their way over to us: movies (a few months late), comic books, magazines, and the *Stars and Stripes* newspaper. But so many familiar facets of life had been left back in the U.S., including fast-food restaurants, drive-in movie theaters, roller rinks, weenie roasts, and penny-candy stores. As we learned over time, there were Spanish substitutes for some of them. But that was just the point—they were substitutes. Not quite like the things we were used to, not exactly what we'd left behind.

While an ancient, majestic culture surrounded us, it wasn't always easy to immerse ourselves in it. Without language fluency, we felt awkward and conspicuous. And many of the Spaniards didn't like GIs or their families because we represented the American government they wanted out of their country. Royal Oaks and the Torrejon Air Base were like peculiar islands upon which we had been cast, and from which we'd occasionally issue forth on adventures into the unfamiliar waters around us.

We were far from miserable, and there were many happy times. Still, curiously, we felt constrained, cordoned off from our homes, country, and extended families, always yearning for the day when we could return. The novelty of this enchanting setting was offset by the loss of freedom that came with being dependents to servicemen, placed on the overseas tour for several years away from our beloved homeland. I suppose our sacrifices made us feel that much more patriotic.

"Hey, look—moving van!"

Mark ran to the edge of our driveway as a white truck lumbered up to our unit with two brawny men in the cab, regarding us with amusement.

"Hola!" one of them called in our direction as a small group collected to watch the action.

The kids in Royal Oaks always found it exciting when someone new moved into the neighborhood, as though they were joining our team and becoming comrades-in-arms.

The broad-shouldered, stout men jumped down, opened the back door, and began carrying boxes and furnishings into the empty first-floor unit.

"Wonder what kind of stuff he's got?" Mark said aloud exactly what I was thinking as we looked at the boxes piling up in the carport.

We always watched these move-in proceedings anxiously, hoping for some clues as to who the kids were: how old, how many, and what fun toys or games they had. I was particularly excited about our new neighbors since I'd learned that Mr. Mazza had a young son, about my age, as well as a teenage daughter exactly Kathy's age—and they'd be right downstairs!

With the constant flux of families into and out of our housing complex, I'd recently lost my good friends Stevie Lothrop, when he went back to Louisiana with his family, and Tom Henner, whose father was retiring from the Air Force and heading back to their hometown on the West Coast. After these two left, Mark became my closest friend, though our interests weren't always perfectly aligned. I liked reading comics and other books, building model ships, planes, and tanks, and playing with miniatures like matchbox cars, electric trains, and toy soldiers. Mark wasn't so captivated by these things, but he liked to play outside with me and catch lizards. His father, a stern man who always wore a white T-shirt and green military pants around the house, had some neat German train sets he'd pull out around Christmas and set up on the living room floor in interlacing patterns with trestles, bridges, and crossings. I loved to lie on the floor and watch them course around the tracks in the dark, the bright headlights glinting along the silver rails.

I also had a bit of a crush on one of Mark's four sisters, Terri, so I liked to go over to his house.

Since our other friends had left, when it came to stalking the gullies, it was really just Mark and me.

"We could use some help down there." I pointed to the open hillsides behind us, and Mark nodded, following my gaze.

There was plenty of room to expand our little lizard-catching band. So I couldn't wait to meet Mr. Mazza and his family, hoping to incorporate his son into our reptile adventures.

Four

When I turned the corner at the bottom of the stairs, I saw a short man with curly, salt-and-pepper hair and an olive complexion; a little stout but not heavy, with a sincere, radiant smile, who'd just pulled up in a black Cadillac. Curiously, he was wearing a suit. It was most unusual to see a military man in a suit and tie, except perhaps on Sundays. Our fathers wore the Air Force working blues to work nearly every day in winter, and khakis in summer. Or, if there was some sort of alert happening on the base, they'd be required to wear what my dad called his "fatigues," a green, baggy ensemble that was meant, I supposed, for combat.

Mr. Mazza instantly fascinated me. I soon learned he was the manager of the Officers' Club at the Air Force Base. This fact evoked earnest admiration. The O Club was "Officer country," the gathering place for those of a higher echelon, and not a place I'd ever go—it had a real sense of importance about it. And our new neighbor was in charge of the establishment!

"Hi, boys," he said, greeting Mark and me cheerfully.

He had a distinct accent, and I later learned he was from New York City. I got the sense when he spoke that he genuinely liked whomever he was speaking to. It wasn't the polite interest of an adult speaking to a child, but held real warmth. There was an instant bond or something. I couldn't have described this coveted trait then, but I could feel it. Many years later, I would understand that certain people simply embrace you, somehow, from the moment they first pronounce your name. My father did not have that gift, and growing up to be much like him, neither do I. But everyone in my family could sense it, and we readily developed an affection and appreciation for a man who exuded such character. I immediately knew, too, that I would like his son. I was sure he'd be just like Mr. Mazza.

"Let me show you something," he called in his already familiar tone. "My son, Mike, has a minibike. Did you guys ever ride a minibike?"

Mr. Mazza made his way around the corner and onto his front porch as he spoke. The movers had already carried most of their goods into their new home. When he returned to the carport, he was pushing a little red motorbike. Looking at us, he grinned broadly. "Who's first, boys?"

I looked at Mark, my eyes wide with surprise and anxiety. I wasn't the most adventurous boy—I'd nearly fainted with fear when my cousin Keith once took me for a ride on his new Honda motorcycle.

"Hang on, Stevie!" I remember Keith calling to me repeatedly over his shoulder as I clung to him with all my might. As we sped along, it had occurred to me that if I let go, I would surely die.

"I'll try it," Mark said, stepping up and grasping the handlebars with cautious enthusiasm.

I watched him climb onto the bike, a little ashamed of my reluctance and now beginning to feel curious. "Maybe," I thought, "I can ride it, too."

Mr. Mazza pulled the cord on the little engine beneath the seat, and it roared to life. His voice boomed over the motor while Mark and I strained to hear him.

"It's really easy—here's the throttle," he called, gunning the engine gently a few times to get us used to the sound.

He turned and pointed toward the end of the long gravel driveway and began pushing Mark on the motorbike in that direction, looking back over his shoulder at me. Suddenly, Mark was under power, and he sped forward on the little red bike, free of all assistance. He bounced along jauntily, apparently in control and having fun, veering this way and that as he headed out to the far end of the driveway, where he steered out of the gravel and around a large oak tree, then made his way back to us near the carport.

"Now, Stevie, you try it," called Mr. Mazza.

I saw the minibike not as an ally or a chance for recreation but rather as a potential enemy to be feared, perhaps even an opportunity for humiliation or injury. To add to my anxiety, not long before this episode I'd lost my cousin Keith when his motorcycle crashed into a truck in Virginia. Still, since Mark had vanquished the little motorbike, I knew I was now required to at least make an attempt to ride it.

"Just sit on it, put your feet on these pegs, rev the throttle, and go!" Mr. Mazza shouted in my ear.

I sat astride the sputtering mechanical beast. Mark had made it look so easy as he drove up and down the driveway that I almost forgot how fearful I was.

A few of the neighborhood kids had drifted over to see what the excitement was about. Standing expectantly beside the driveway, they looked on, waiting to see me master this little machine. There were no gears, for which I was thankful, just a throttle and a hand brake. Smelling the exhaust and hearing the chattering of the tiny two-stroke engine, I began to believe I could ride the way Mark had. Leaning forward, I turned to Mr. Mazza, who beamed at me, no doubt elated that the local kids were having so much fun with the minibike he'd purchased for his son.

"C'mon, Steve . . . pop a wheelie!" Mark was a bit more enthusiastic than I was.

I set my teeth in sober determination and pulled hard on the throttle. Too hard. The bike lurched into motion, and I was off balance from the start. I careened this way and that, stones flying from under the back tire while alarmed children ducked and ran for cover. Blue-black smoke swirled around me, and I was suddenly too terrified to continue, yet too embarrassed to stop. By the time I reached the driveway's end, I was afraid to look back. Turning abruptly, I crossed to the other side, bordered by a fairly steep downhill into Stevie Lothrop's yard, a furrowed, sandy hillside. Certain I could pull out of the turn, I again hit the gas, hoping to preserve the illusion that I had some degree of control. I leaned into the curve so much that the bike threatened to go over. The back wheel suddenly spun out on the loose rocks, and I found myself over the side of the embankment, skidding down the hill with no ability to steer the bike. It fell over, but somehow, I remained standing on trembling legs.

"Are you all right, Stevie?" Though I wasn't hurt, Mr. Mazza was already trotting out to my rescue.

This event defined a self-fulfilling cycle of defeat I'd experienced many times: The process began with anxiety, moved on to loss of confidence, led to a half-hearted attempt at some complex task, and finally resulted in a predictable flop. Each such episode led to a more profound fear of failure.

With reddened cheeks and perhaps a glint of a frustrated tear in my eye, I hung my head and walked back to my carport where Mark stood watching me with his humble smile. The crowd had dissipated, for which I was grateful.

Mr. Mazza walked along with me and patted me warmly on the back. "Don't worry, you'll get better. When Mike gets here, you guys can ride all you want. They should be coming later this evening."

"Thanks, Mr. Mazza," we called as he stored the minibike.

He was a kind man, and I already sensed we were lucky to have acquired him as a neighbor. I anticipated that the rest of his family would be just as upbeat, optimistic, and friendly.

"Don't forget the pool passes!" Mark was already running down the hill to get his trunks on and grab a towel.

It was about a mile and a half to the pool. There wasn't any good way to get around Royal Oaks except to walk or bike, since most families only had one car, which was gone every day when dads went to work on base. Biking in the streets was dangerous, so we mostly confined our riding to our driveways. We usually walked to school, the movies, or the pool. On this sunny afternoon, we made our way quickly along the hot sidewalks, watching the walls for scurrying lizards.

"Are you ready for school?" I asked, knowing what his answer was likely to be.

Mark ran ahead a few steps alongside one of the many granite walls in Royal Oaks that lined our roads and held hillsides back. He snapped his towel playfully against the wall and skipped a few steps.

"No, I'm not ready. But my mom sure is—she bought me some new shirts and some pencils and pens and notebooks, but I wish we had a few more weeks. I want summer to last all year-round, don't you?" His dark eyes met mine, and his grin was more pronounced.

"Well, yeah, except for Christmas. We have to have it cold and snowy at Christmas."

It had snowed only once in the three years I had lived in Spain, amounting to no more than a dusting.

"Tomorrow afternoon I'll be counting the minutes until school is over. It's like a prison."

Mark contemplated this as we walked along, and briefly almost lost his perpetual smile. "Well, it's worse for me," he said. "I've gotta get up even earlier to catch the bus, and I can't walk with you and Mauro anymore."

"Yeah, we'll miss you. What time do you get home?"

Mark was moving up to middle school.

"I think about four. It doesn't sound too fun. Terri and Rita told me that the teachers are a lot harder out there."

The elementary school for those of us on Royal Oaks was right in the housing area. After fifth grade, everyone had to take a bus out to the base, where the middle school and high school were located. The base was only a half-hour ride, but somehow being herded together with older kids and then shuttled to someplace distant to go to school seemed foreign and depressing. No one relished the transition; our small school just down the hill was inviting and familiar, while the schools on base seemed forbidding, even threatening. I understood why even Mark had trouble smiling at the prospect.

"It's still our day."

"Yeah," he countered. "Let's just have fun. School is a whole day away."

We cut through a few yards, finally arriving at the parking lot in front of the pool. I snapped Mark with my towel and ran down the hill, he chasing after me, both of us laughing and trying to fend off the sharp sting of the towels as we cavorted.

Entering the pool compound, I was greeted immediately by the smell of chlorine and grilled hamburgers from the snack bar. Little more could excite a ten-year-old boy encountering those intermixed aromas—they were the very essence of summertime.

We staked out our turf, unrolled our towels on the lukewarm grass, and trotted to the edge of the pool. I dipped a toe in the water. Mark waited until just the right moment, when my balance was compromised and my eyes averted, to give a firm push against my back, and into the water I went. Bobbing to the surface, I wiped my eyes and called to him to jump in. On the last day of August, the water was cool, but it felt pleasant enough on that sunny afternoon, and Mark was diving in beside me in a moment.

"Race you to the deep end," I called, and the contest was on.

We were back on our towels a few minutes later, shivering and dripping.

"You think he'll wanna catch lizards?" I asked.

"Who?" Mark asked, looking up at the cloudless sky, shielding his eyes from the sun.

"Mike—you know, the new kid, downstairs from me."

"Yeah. Oh, yeah. Everybody likes to catch lizards."

"Mauro doesn't."

"That's cause his mom won't let him. She's Portuguese. She doesn't like him to go out in the gullies. He can't even play baseball. She won't let him do anything."

I sighed in sad recognition. Mauro was a good friend even though he wasn't allowed to do much with us.

At a quarter till five, the lifeguards whistled us out and announced the closure for the season. We were OK with it, though, having lamented, brooded, and reminisced; having dived, raced, splashed, and challenged; having reclined, daydreamed, snacked, and even dozed.

With our towels now saturated, we were much better at snapping each other on the way home. The stinging welts kept us howling in pain and darting quickly across the lawns and sidewalks.

"Take that . . . and that . . . and that!" I shouted as I ran along the driveway toward my carport, Mark running backward and giggling, just out of reach of my towel.

We arrived, breathless, to see the new boy standing beside his car, looking at us wondrously, unsure of how to react.

"Are you Mike?" Mark asked, red-faced and puffing.

"Yeah—what are you guys playing?"

I was mature enough to shake hands by this point, as was Mark. After introductions all around, we explained our little towel-snapping chase game.

"It gets us to the pool a lot faster," my friend explained.

Mike was a little shorter than Mark and me but more substantial, with a stockier build. Like Mark, he had very dark hair. His father's Italian heritage had provided dark, round eyes and a slightly swarthy complexion. To me, he seemed confident, always ready to laugh, and able to take charge socially. In these ways, he was much like his father. I instantly liked him.

"I wiped out on your minibike," I confessed.

"That's OK—my dad told me about it. What happened?"

I pointed to the end of the driveway, where the short downhill led off to the left, toward what had once been the Lothrops' quarters. Mark tried to suppress his ever-present grin, and Mike looked at me, gently shaking his head as he tried to imagine the misadventure.

"Don't worry," he offered, "I'll teach you how to ride it."

I felt a warm satisfaction from that exchange. I was excited as I realized I would be friends with this new boy who happened to live right beneath me. I was rather pious at that point in my life, and as I lay awake on my bed in the evening, I thanked God for granting me a new playmate, along with all the other aspects of my life that I routinely thanked Him for.

My dad tiptoed quietly past my room that evening. "You're not asleep yet?" The door was open, and my light was still on.

"Not yet. Will you read to me?" I asked hopefully.

He paused, given the lateness of the hour. "Tomorrow's the first day of school."

"I know, Dad . . . Please? It'll help me sleep."

"OK—but just for a few minutes."

We had a wonderful symbiosis at bedtime, my father and I. He would read aloud to me in exchange for my gently rubbing his scalp. At that age, it felt natural and even satisfying to touch my father as he lay beside me, reading. It was our daily time to bond since he'd returned from Vietnam. His absence from my life for twelve long months led me to relish his company even more than I did before his deployment. I had yearned constantly to see him during that solitary year. Aimless and displaced, moody and disconsolate, I had experienced what it was like, even if temporarily, for a boy to grow up without a father figure.

However much I loved my grandfather and my Uncle Al, with whom we were living that year, the two could not make up for the loss of my father. My funk deepened when, at one point, the entire second-grade class at St. Basil's Elementary was required to attend the funeral of a classmate's mother, who had died of cancer. I remembered the shiver of fear I felt upon seeing the casket; after that funeral mass, I would sometimes awaken in the middle of the night, terrified that I would be attending my own father's funeral. The dread of his death haunted me until the day I saw him at the airport, thin and jaundiced. He arrived with a pencil-thin mustache ("shave it off!" we demanded) and a sallow, sickly complexion. But there he was, my loving father, returned intact from the war.

During that lonely time in Pittsburgh, I felt as if I had been a mere apparition, stumbling through a dreadful tale created by someone else and always awaiting the one event that would restore me to a meaningful existence. Within a week of my father's return from Vietnam, we bade farewell to my relatives and were bound for Madrid. Thereafter, Dad's love and attention were all the more important to me. His reading in my room was a cherished gesture. Not only did he share his time and effort, but also his wisdom and gentle personality. We frequently interrupted the reading to talk about the day's events, what might have been bothering me at the time, how I was getting along with a friend, or even what I planned to do with all those lizards.

In the dim light from the lamp on my dresser, my father did as much for the maturation of my thought processes with his discussion and simple readings as any classroom work ever did.

"What is it tonight, Tom?"

He called me Tom sometimes—which wasn't in any way part of my name—because he had been a great fan of 1950s Yankees pitcher Tommy Davis. I liked that he called me by a name that had belonged to a beloved major league player in his past.

"*Ants and Bees*," I said, holding up the softbound picture book.

"Ahh, here's where we left off," he noted. "'While worker bees devote their lives to collecting nectar, constructing the hive, caring for the young, and defending the queen, the drones have but one important function.'"

We read a few more paragraphs, and I interrupted. "Why do you think drones do that? What a lousy life—born just to mate with the queen and then die? And most of them never get to mate at all. Why don't they just fly off and enjoy some nectar from flowers, you know, and leave the hive?"

My father thought for a moment. "I don't think that they get much of a choice. It's kind of an instinct—they wouldn't feel right if they just left the rest of the bees in the hive. A drone wouldn't be fulfilling its purpose in life."

Nodding drowsily, I considered that as he closed the book and wished me a good night. My lids were heavy as the room went dark. But I kept thinking, as I drifted off to sleep, about the importance of having a purpose in life, like a drone, a queen, or a worker bee.

Five

The first day of fifth grade dawned bright and clear. As always, I was sleepy-eyed and grumpy; I was not a morning person. My mother, however, resolved to compensate for my irritability with her effusive, sunny outlook.

"Good morning, sunshine. Time to get up!" she called cheerfully, throwing my door open and briskly pulling back the curtains on my window.

Such artificial pleasantries served only to agitate me. I groaned and rolled over, intent upon exploiting every possible moment of snooze I could manage, tenting the covers to block the light that was now streaming in, then pulling the pillow over my head to block out the image of my mother.

She was undeterred and moved to the next step in our carefully choreographed morning dance: pulling the pillow off me, raising her voice to a higher pitch, describing the day's weather, and finally pulling down my blanket.

Deprived of darkness, warmth, and silence, I capitulated. But not happily. Growling, I rolled out of bed, sitting on the edge.

"It's the first day of school! Don't you want to get there and meet all the new kids?"

I shook my head, hoping she'd exit after seeing I had adopted an upright position, which would give me a few more minutes to topple over and sleep.

But she persisted, laying my clothes on the bed, demanding that I get dressed. There was no resisting her assault of effervescence, but I knew she would become weary of it all in the coming months. This face-off was just round one.

"C'mon—your friends will be here in twenty minutes. You need to wash up, dress, brush your teeth, and get some breakfast."

That sounded like a lot to do in twenty minutes.

But the warm Spanish sunlight filled my room and brightened my outlook. I began to experience, not dread, but the exuberance of returning to someplace familiar. I'd done everything I could to ward off any consideration of returning to school: ignoring every reference to the place, shunning any discussion, and purposely channeling my thoughts against it. However, as with all appointments with destiny, the moment of truth had arrived. While I had been busy accentuating the negatives of returning to school, TC's perspective kept creeping into my mind: "It's still fun to see all your friends and get to know your teacher. And meet new friends."

Somehow, her upbeat, enthusiastic outlook had sublimated itself into my own attitude. Now that avoidance, aversion, and flight were all but impossible, I sensed a strange yearning to catch up with the friends I hadn't seen all summer, to meet the new kids that had just moved in, and even to see my new teacher, whose name I knew but with whom I was unfamiliar.

On that first morning, Mike walked to school with Mauro and me. We took our shortcut down through the gullies and across some backyards to the road just above the baseball fields and down the big hill.

"I had a lot of friends in my school back home. Most of them played baseball. You guys have Little League here?" Mike entertained us the whole way to school with stories about his sports teams back in Alabama, about his little dog, Frenchie, and about his flamboyant father. "We had a really good team back in Alabama. Nobody could get hits against our best pitcher."

Mike wasn't threatened by new circumstances. He was excited about going to a new school in a new place; I already felt admiration for him.

On his first day at the school I had been attending for several years, he was already more extroverted and confident than I was. Sometimes my own reticence bewildered me. This reluctance just seemed to be part of my makeup; my father's endless admonitions to "be aggressive" and my continuous introspection didn't seem to change anything.

After walking down the hill, we lined up on the playground, preparing to go into the school class-by-class and line-by-line. Our lives were quite regimented, but as a group of military brats, we didn't question this. Perhaps we sensed that, collectively, our fathers suffered the same fate in their inspections and formations.

Shuffling forward, we entered the school, headed for our homerooms, and prepared for the drudgery of the next nine months. There were old friends in my class: Jay, tall and slim and a bit reluctant to speak, though always approachable and friendly; Dino, who spoke fluent Spanish and lived with his Spanish mother and American father in Madrid; James Neal, studious and efficient, with whom I'd put together a little cookbook for our Mother's Day project last year; and Mauro, my neighbor.

"Hi, Steven!" I heard a friendly voice call. To my surprise, TC was in my class. I tried not to look too overjoyed or run over to her; rather, I acknowledged her with a smile and a noncommittal wave. But in truth, I was delighted to see her.

And there were new kids: James Brock, who was a bit gruff and mysterious, wearing a trench coat, along with a fedora; Louis, who was lean, tall and stoic, spoke with a French accent, and had come from Saigon. There was a pale kid with short blond hair named Stocker, who I knew from baseball, with a reputation for fierce competitiveness and a great pitching arm. Oh, and a girl named Kelly Schulz.

"Hey, Kelly," I said softly when I saw her looking over in my direction. But I was in a crowd, and I really didn't know if she was looking at me specifically.

Her father was a lieutenant colonel, and he was also my dentist. In my admiring eyes, Kelly was simply lovely: brunette, blue-eyed, fair-skinned. She had a round, pretty face and an enchanting smile. I'd had a bit of a crush on her the prior school year—from afar, of course. Unfortunately, my friend Mauro now claimed her as his girl. It was an odd sort of arrangement that I didn't quite understand. Both acknowledged she was his girlfriend even though they rarely spoke to one another or even paid much attention to each other. I would have loved to work my way over and talk to her, but I was not one to compete for the attention of a pretty girl. Shyness and reluctance were integral to my persona, and I was well aware that the most attractive girl in the class does not fawn over a boy imbued with such traits. Besides, Mauro was a good friend, and I thought he was pretty cool. So I admired her in silence, secretly overjoyed that she was close by, and that I could distract myself with secretive glances at her throughout the day.

After we entered the classroom, a few minutes passed, and the uproar that marked our joyous reunion suddenly gave way to respectful silence. A small, wiry man with curly, close-cropped gray hair strode into the room. He was impeccably dressed in a gray suit, and as he walked to the front, he looked at the students on each side of the center aisle, smiling graciously and nodding as if he'd known us all for years. He bore the wrinkles of advanced age but exuded a youthful enthusiasm. There was no sternness about him, but he somehow commanded our respect. The entire class was briefly mesmerized.

"Good morning. I'm Mr. Walden," he said, pointing to his name, which was neatly printed on the blackboard: Gene C. Walden.

"I have a lot for you to do this year," he continued, "and it's going to be so much fun. We're going to learn many things. But I also expect *you* to work—hard. We'll make posters and go on field trips and learn Spanish songs and Mexican dances. We'll make books about what we learn and improve our reading and arithmetic. I want you to read a book every single week. Then, I want you to do a book report on what you've read."

Bewilderment and dismay appeared on the faces of my classmates as he pronounced these many requirements. My eyebrows lifted. Mr. Walden continued to name projects we'd be involved in, and his attitude left no doubt that he meant all the things he said.

Inside, I felt a little thrill: Mr. Walden was throwing down the gauntlet.

By the time our lunch period rolled around and we filed out of the room toward the cafeteria, followed by recess on the blacktop, Gene C. Walden had created a spell, which settled gently upon the whole class. The grumblings and misgivings of my classmates had given way to acceptance and even enthusiasm. In those first few hours, we'd received a math lesson, started our reading modules, related current events, discussed a field trip to the Royal Palace in Madrid, and picked out cartoons to draw as large posters for the first-graders, who were in a separate building. We would decorate their classrooms and hallways with our lighthearted renderings as our first art project.

"Steven," he asked me, walking past my desk, "how did you end up picking Snuffy Smith as your cartoon?"

I felt honored, somehow, that he asked.

"He's one of my dad's favorites," I told him, "I think because his family is from the country, just like Snuffy's."

He laughed with delight, but not just politely. Rather, he let go a truly joyful guffaw. Composing himself, he suggested that my father's family might not like the comparison since the Snuffy Smith clan was short on sophistication. Still, I told him there were some pretty strong similarities, and he liked that even more.

With his charm, warmth, and sense of humor, he rapidly won over the children in my class, one by one, gently teasing stories out of them, offering an insight or an observation that was just personal enough. Despite all the work he seemed to want from us, he nonetheless gained our trust, affection, and devotion.

At the end of that first day, I knew he would be the best teacher I'd ever have.

Six

Mauro and I continually praised Mr. Walden as we walked home from school with Mike, who was equally enthusiastic about his teacher, Mr. Snyder. It was a bit of one-upmanship, but Mauro and I carried the day, since our new instructor had promised too many good things for either of us to consider giving way. And, after all, we were upperclassmen. It was the first time I had ever argued with someone about who was fortunate enough to have the best teacher.

We were almost home at this point, cutting through the gullies just below our quarters. I figured the argument was going nowhere; Mike wasn't budging.

"Hey, you wanna catch lizards?" I asked, turning to face the two of them.

Mauro wasn't allowed to play in the gullies, so he gave us a friendly "goodbye" and off he went, picking his way along the paths and across the ravines toward the unit he called home. When I stood on our terraza, I could see Mauro's quarters across the expanse of sandy terrain and sagebrush that lay between us. Our families had the same arrangement: an elevated porch facing the wide patch of undeveloped land that ran down the slope. Sometimes, he and I would be out on the terraza at the same time, gazing down the hill, and we would wave to each other from our lofty perches.

I gave Mike a few pointers and explained, as best I could, the objects of our hunt and why catching lizards was an essential aspect of living in Royal Oaks.

"They're perfect," I said admiringly. "When you pick one up and look at it, it has all these tiny parts: eyes like those small colored balls on the end of your mom's sewing pins, a mouth and tongue that seem so little that they can barely eat with them, toes and claws so fine you almost can't feel them when they wrap around your finger. They're like tiny dinosaurs. And they're out here, tons of them for us to catch."

Mike was mildly interested. "What do we *do* with them?"

I was reluctant to admit to Mike that we had some problems once they were in captivity. "Well, we find different things to feed them—you know, like bugs or hamburger. And we make some really cool terrariums for them to live in, with sand, sticks, and rocks to make them feel at home . . . so they won't mind being up on my terraza."

"Does that really work?" Mike asked, getting right to the point.

"Well, yeah. For a little while, anyway. But when it comes to eating, it's not so great. So sometimes we have to let them go again."

That didn't seem to bother him. And so, the hunt was on.

I led him down one of our most frequently used paths, which led to a trench some five or six feet deep, and ten feet across, an arroyo that bore the scars of the torrent of rushing water that was channeled there during our infrequent rains. Stones littered the bottom of the ditch, along with some old, rusty cans in which the paper wasps liked to nest, so we avoided disturbing them. We scrambled across and up the other side. Sagebrush surrounded us as we followed the path a few more yards, its thick scent overlying the gullies and most of the Royal Oaks, like a sticky, sweet netting.

"Over there," I said to Mike, pointing toward a flicker of movement in the dry leaves, accompanied by a soft rustling sound I'd learned to pay attention to.

As I gestured, Mike hustled to the other side of a collection of small sagebrush shrubs. I stood fast, and sure enough, a fine specimen emerged toward me, racing at full speed.

"Here, over here," I called.

Mike surprised me with his quickness, rapidly coming up behind the lizard. Just as it raced out of its cover and across the path, I bent forward and quickly scooped it up.

"Got him, got him!" I yelled, and Mike arrived, panting, by my side.

"Check him out," I said excitedly. "It's a rat-tail!"

The small reptile was nearly motionless in my grasp, eyes fearfully turning this way and that, and its heart visibly palpitating through the loose skin of its throat.

"The rat-tails are gray with a reddish stripe down the side, and all the way down that long tail." I spoke as though I'd studied lizards for years. But my knowledge actually came from a few books we'd checked out from the base library.

"Can I hold him?"

I handed the lizard over to his waiting hands, which closed carefully around our captive. Mike studied him in some detail, impressed at the delicacy of his diminutive form, as we all were. How could something so tiny and seemingly so vulnerable survive in these dangerous, barren lands? We would count their spots or stripes, peer into their tiny black eyes, and marvel at the precise engineering of the toes and claws. They usually became quite docile as we handled them, probably accepting their fate and inevitable demise. It was difficult to imagine what such a small creature might have perceived in this situation, unfolding as it did in the hands of giants.

I looked up and saw a grin on Mike's face. I was sure he was now one of the chosen few in our hunting circle. It was a small group, to be sure, and very select. But now we were expanded by one. There was a hint of satisfaction in his features, which pleased me—I had impressed the kid with the mini-bike.

"What now?" he asked, clinging to the frightened reptile as we trudged up the hill toward the white, institutional-looking building we called home.

"Well, I have some others from yesterday up on my terraza, in a bucket. Let's introduce them and see if they get along."

I grabbed Mike's bookbag, and we walked the rest of the way up the hill and then up the stairs to the terrace.

"What's that?" My sister asked, peering over the railing as we came up.

"It's a lizard, that's what. A rat-tail," I said, knowing she'd make some smart-aleck comment that reflected her lack of appreciation of our hobby.

"Gross. Gross-e-osa. Who would name a lizard after a rat?" She laughed with her newfound friend, Anna-Marie, dark-haired and pretty. The two had just come home on the bus from the first day of high school on base. It struck me as pretty special that our downstairs neighbors had a girl Kathy's age and a boy my age. The arrangement promised to make the next year a lot of fun for all four of us.

"Kathy," I heard my mom call from inside. "We're leaving at six o'clock to go into Madrid."

"Not me. Can I stay at Marie's? She's going to show me all her makeup."

"Are you sure it's OK with Mrs. Mazza?" my mother replied, careful to avoid burdening the new neighbors with her children this early in our relationship.

Maria nodded furiously as the two stood outside the front door on the narrow walkway that led from the terraza to the entryway.

"Yeah, Mom. Marie asked."

I looked at Mike. We both frowned. They hadn't asked—we knew our sisters too well. They were already engaged in playing one set of parents against the other. But if I could ditch Kathy for an evening visit to Madrid, it would be most desirable. She always wanted to cut our outings short, to get home again and talk on the phone.

"Steve, are you out there?"

I replied, waiting for instructions.

"We're leaving in half an hour for Manuel's to look for chandelier parts, then to the *calle* to get supper. Maybe we'll stop at Woolworths afterward."

It was always a treat to go into Madrid. We called it going to "the calle," the Spanish name for street, and we had a routine: shopping, eating, and strolling the streets of old Madrid. My father had taken up chandelier-building as a hobby when we moved to Spain. Fluted glass arms, crystal teardrops, and all manner of fancy translucent doodads were everywhere in Spain. Chandeliers, candelabras, and sconces encrusted with glittering appendages were an essential part of Spanish history and culture. So Dad meticulously combed through little tables of trinkets and crystalline accessories at flea markets and in little towns. He had also met a few vendors in Madrid, some of whom supplied him at the *rastro*, a massive outdoor flea market that took over the city's old quarter on Sunday mornings. One of these vendors, Manuel, lived deep in the old part of the city, and we visited his house every few months. After we looked at the antique glassware and perhaps purchased a crystal accessory or two, we'd go off to shop at a market. Afterward, we'd head to a bodega, a Spanish tavern, and eat tapas for supper. To a GI, this was a cheap way to feed the family.

"They look pretty sad," Mike said, bringing me back to the moment. He was peering down at the trio of lizards lying in the plastic bucket on our elevated porch.

The three brownies lay motionless, equidistant, at the bottom of the makeshift terrarium. They cocked their heads, observing us with their beady eyes, but otherwise were completely at rest, their breathing barely perceptible. Into this unfriendly arena, we dumped the rat-tail. One of the brownies shifted a bit, leaving his long tail furled beneath him. The rat-tail promptly established himself in a similar position of immobility. A pile of dead flies and raw hamburger lay untouched in the center of the bucket amid some small stones and sticks we'd placed there. A tiny bowl of water appeared likewise undisturbed.

"I don't get it," I said gloomily to my new friend. "We work so hard to give them a good place to live. Then they just sit there. They don't eat, they don't drink. They don't even chase the crickets or ants if you put them in there."

Mike looked uncertainly at me. "Maybe that's not what they eat?"

"Well of course it's what they eat," I insisted, hoping to establish my expertise.

Hadn't I caught lizards for three years? Hadn't I gone out of my way to learn about their markings, habits, and preferences? How could I let a new guy question me? I was defensive, perhaps even snotty, and suddenly aware of my attitude—he was trying to help, and I was acting as if threatened.

I backtracked. "Yeah, maybe you're right. I know they eat meat, not plants. They surely like bugs, but what kind? I figured any meat-eater likes hamburger. But even big lizards can't eat a cow!"

We both laughed, and the ill feelings I'd created quickly dissolved.

"Let's give them time to make friends," I said, putting the bucket down.

"How long do you keep them?" he asked as we walked back toward the steps.

"Well, a couple days, usually. My dad says if they don't start to eat by then, it's time to let them out again. He says they could starve."

Mike's mom called out the window from their kitchen, probably anxious to hear about his first day at school.

"Bye," he said, gazing down at the lizards. "Can I come see them tomorrow?"

"Course," I said, pleased that he'd asked. "And we can go catch some more."

I went into my room and changed out of my school clothes. My mom would've given me an earful if she'd seen me scurrying around after lizards in the gullies in my good pants and shirt. It was still *mucho calor* outside, a hot Spanish afternoon, so I put on shorts to go into Madrid.

I heard the front door open, and I knew my dad was home.

"Hey, Dad, we caught a rat-tailed racerunner!" I shouted, running out to greet him.

He tried to muster some genuine enthusiasm, raising his eyebrows. "Wow. And what exactly is a rat-tailed racerunner?"

I figured he'd have memorized the most common lizard types by then, but he always seemed surprised when I told him what we'd caught. Dad was in his working blues, neat and officious. From the shiny shoes, which I sometimes helped him spit-shine, to the floppy garrison cap, which he pulled off and stuck in his belt as he came in, he was the picture of the military man. The "hats on, hats off" habit was reflexive for those in uniform, and spoke of an old-fashioned politeness. Airmen didn't wear their covers indoors, and they always wore them outside. I hurried onto the porch and brought the bucket to the front door to show him the prized new acquisition.

"Hmmm . . . that's quite an impressive set of lizards. But they don't look very happy."

"Yeah, I know. We still can't get them to eat anything."

"Well, you've cooped them up. They're free-running animals. Being stuck in a bucket is definitely a step down."

"But Dad, they just got in there. I think they need a little time. They'll get used to it."

"Steve," he said a bit more sternly, "in a little time, they'll be dead. Remember what happened last year?"

I remembered. We lost two sets of lizards, who also wouldn't eat. My father was not highly educated, but he had a subtle wisdom, particularly when it came to animals and natural things. Maybe because he'd grown up on a farm among people who were simple but sensible, hard-working, and earnest. He seemed to know about creatures, plants, weather, and human nature. I knew he would chide me until I turned the lizards back into the gullies.

Running to my room, I quickly combed my hair and changed clothes, anticipating our little family trip. I frowned at myself in the mirror, disappointed that even after several years of trying to take care of our lizards I could not unravel the mystery of their diet.

Seven

Our first stop when we drove into the city was often in a downtrodden neighborhood—or at least it seemed so to me. The homes were small, two-story row houses, tightly packed together, set back from the street, with small courtyards in front, protected by fences or iron gates. Many of these front spaces were filled with debris of one sort or another. Not garbage, just stuff people weren't using, it appeared. After parking on the impossibly narrow street, we walked a few paces to a rusty metal door in an equally rusty metal fence. It was solid, not a fence you could see through, except at the very top, where there was a metal lattice running across to let some light into the courtyard, I supposed. It was a bit foreboding, as you couldn't see anything beyond the deteriorating partition. My father banged on the aged metal several times in succession, and a few moments later, the gate slowly creaked open.

A stooped, grizzled elderly man with white whiskers blinked at us through thick glasses. Though it took a few seconds for him to recognize us, he smiled, and a flicker of warmth came into his deep-set eyes.

"Manuel! Hola!" my dad said, warmly extending his hand.

"Hola, hola!" Manuel retorted, apparently pleased to see us.

Manuel didn't get a lot of American visitors, I figured, or maybe any visitors at all.

"Hola, Manuel," I said, as he patted me on the head.

"Maria!" the old man called, summoning his wife.

An equally aged, and almost equally stooped, woman came shuffling out of the house, bowing and nodding pleasantly to welcome us. There was a lot of hand gesturing.

"Antiguidades? Crystallidades?" Dad asked. I wasn't sure those were actual words, but they seemed to carry the appropriate meaning.

Manuel knew well enough why we were there.

The old man nodded amicably and gestured toward the front door. His wife went in and soon returned with an enamel basin filled with various glass, metal, and crystal pieces. This time, she was accompanied by a very short man, probably no taller than I, wearing some stained pants and a tattered sweater. He walked unevenly a few paces behind her, as if hesitant to see us but still anxious to make an appearance, like a small, bashful child. This was Manuel's son, who, my father had once explained to me, had a birth defect. I had been terrified of him when I was younger—he brayed sometimes, like a donkey, as he tried to communicate with his mother and father. Since it was difficult to understand him, he would be quite persistent, becoming louder with each attempt to speak. His mother and father were gentle and engaging with him, introducing him each time to us, hushing him when necessary, but keeping him involved in the proceedings.

I stayed close to my dad, but I gestured to the young man, who was probably in his thirties or early forties. His face lit up as he recognized me.

"Mira, señor," Manuel said, inviting us to look at his wares, sifting through the basin.

In turn, he held up various glass adornments for candelabras, sconces, and chandeliers. Most were fancy versions of teardrops in a variety of shapes: some flat, some round, others tubular or even pyramidal. As he presented each one, Manuel looked expectantly at my father's face for approval. None of the pieces fit with the chandelier my father was building at the moment, and he had neither the money nor the space to keep an inventory for future projects. He smiled deferentially but shook his head.

"No quiere estes crystallidades?" the wife asked, tilting her head in an inquisitive way, affirming that my father did not want to buy any of the pieces.

"QUIERE!" shouted her son in his forceful, abrasive voice, startling me. His mother hushed him kindly, and we turned to leave. Manuel didn't have the right parts this time, but we'd be back in a few weeks. My father had managed a description, with hand gestures and a drawing of what he was looking for, and the man had nodded agreeably, as though he knew just where to procure such pieces.

"Muchas gracias," my father said graciously, and I echoed his words.

Our family was far from wealthy, at least by U.S. standards, but I was struck by the humility of these people and their surroundings. I wondered what they ate for their supper, and if they had enough food. It bothered me that we didn't find anything to purchase—I wanted to help them somehow. But we returned regularly, as Manuel and his wife well knew, and perhaps on the next occasion there would be a treasure or two in that basin. We would sometimes see Manuel on Sundays when we went to the *rastro*, at the table where he sold his goods among the many hundreds of other hawkers and dealers; I think it made my father feel a bit of a sophisticate to speak with him on familiar terms when we encountered him there.

The iron gate clanged shut behind us, and we heard Manuel's wife utter a timid, "Adios, señor."

Dad and I found my mother waiting patiently in the Peugeot, and off we went to the potato chip factory. Entering the unremarkable, weather-worn warehouse, we were greeted by the heady aroma of roasted nuts and frying potatoes. Bags of their specialties were stacked up on the counter, warm and greasy.

"Uno de este y uno de este," I requested, pointing at one bag of each.

"Cien pesetas," said the young woman behind the counter, who was as oil-stained as the foodstuffs she sold. She was unimpressed by my broken Spanish and looked hot and bored. Secretly, I hoped she was getting off work soon so she could get out of there.

It was just a short walk, then, to the little bodega we had visited for the past few years. We stopped in for a cheap meal probably once or twice a month. Going out to dinner, even in the inexpensive parts of town, wasn't something we could do often. Though we weren't well known there, we sometimes recognized the bartenders, who would return our greetings, uttering a friendly call. This was one of those nights.

"Eh-hola, señor. Cómo está usted?" he called out to my father as we entered.

Spanish men typically spoke only to the man of the family, at least at first. The bartender was broad, stout, and very strong-looking, with a ready smile that revealed a number of crooked and missing teeth. He stood much of the time with his hands on the counter and his big shoulders hunched forward while he talked to the patrons, most of whom he was familiar with. Reaching under the counter, he started us off with a platter of the customary complementary Spanish olives.

Olives were a greeting there, the equivalent of a pineapple in other parts of the world, a sign of welcome. I had learned to love them, salty and meaty as they were.

Dad ordered our typical fare: skewers of grilled lamb meat, charred and juicy, called *pinchos morunos*, along with a plate of roasted, diced potatoes covered with a spicy orange sauce, which the Spaniards termed *patatas bravas*. With some crusty bread, the olives, and a cold bottle of Coke, the tapas made for a substantial and delicious meal.

I stood happily beside my parents in the tavern; two years prior, I'd been awkward and shy in the same setting. It would have been unheard of in the U.S., but as I looked around, I saw many young families dining at the small tables in the bar. The children, like the adults, sipped beer and wine, and ate from small, shared plates. There was usually a soccer game on the screen on a small television in the back of the bar, and when the Madrid team was playing, everyone in the place was riveted by the fuzzy black-and-white images.

My father didn't let me sip his beer at my age, but he seemed to approve of the family-oriented lifestyle around us. The bar was not filled with angry, dissolute, depressed old men escaping from spouses, work, or debt. Or with revelers drinking too much and making fools of themselves. Rather, it was filled with close-knit families and happy people who celebrated with friends and loved ones out on the town, made more sanguine by the joy of subtle alcoholic inebriation. And this wasn't a display of weekend escapism or a special celebration—this occurred every night, in every bodega in Madrid. After a one-hour stroll through the streets in the early evening with their neighbors, people came together to break bread, sip wine, tell stories, and laugh it up. The workaday existence became a distant memory, while life was simply celebrated until late in the evening.

And each morning, apparently, the Spaniards suffered through work after the revelry of the night before, lumbering home for lunch to eat a large midday meal, and then take a healthy nap. Evening once again brought the late-day stroll and the delightful social scene. This was the way of the Spanish people, the daily affirmation of work-life balance, organized around socializing, beer, wine, and modest amounts of fresh and flavorful food. It was quite different from the life I knew back in the United States.

Eight

"It's here!" I called out at the top of my lungs, bounding through the kitchen with joy.

"Wait—let me see!" My sister espied the book in my hand and tried to catch me as I raced around the table.

The Christmas season came early in Royal Oaks—or perhaps I should say, the Christmas-wishing season. Sometime late in September, the JC Penney and Sears and Roebuck catalogs mysteriously appeared. I suppose they came through the mail, but to me, their arrival was heaven sent. We children sometimes felt captive on our housing complex, without a single store outside of a mini-mart and the fruteria. And when we went to the Air Force base, we were restricted to shopping a narrow range of American toys and games stocked in a small section of the Base Exchange known as "Toyland." So we anticipated the annual catalog display of colorful, exciting holiday distractions with a fervor I had not known in my prior life back in the U.S. How we fantasized about our counterparts in the States taking trips to department stores, sitting on Santa's lap, walking in a daze through crowded aisles brimming with the very latest toys!

"Me first. Let me look at it. I'll give it to you tonight."

That seemed fair enough to Kathy, and she allowed me to sit and fantasize for the next hour.

Whether my mother and father had any desire to peruse these catalogs, I don't know. We treated them as our own special invitations from

Santa, and I'm certain this was true for most of the families around us. I would sit quietly, sometimes with a friend, at other times by myself, staring with wide, desiring eyes at the glossy pages of the toy section, carefully dog-earing and making lists, referencing and cross-referencing the index, noting the page numbers and writing them down slowly and legibly lest I miscommunicate my fondest desires. The sections with trains, slot-cars, miniature soldiers, and space toys were particularly heavily researched. Mike, Mark, and Mauro were as thrilled as I was to see the catalogs, and we frequently compared notes regarding what we wanted. But I was sometimes secretive with my selections, concerned that if we all wanted the same thing, perhaps Santa couldn't come through.

In this particular year, I was determined to expand the small model village I'd arranged around my electric train set. Accessories for trains were high on my Christmas list, supplemented by further acquisitions from the small selection of German-made model structures in the Base Exchange.

"Look, Mom," I said, interrupting her housework to call attention to yet another addition to the list.

Bent over the washing machine, she turned from her laundry and regarded me with a look of impatience. Having spent years working in retail at Joseph Horne's and Sears and Roebuck department stores, she was not enthused about the prospect of the holidays, particularly in the waning days of September.

"I have everything marked, and I made a list with page numbers, see?"

Standing up, she gave me her full attention. Duly impressed, she read down the list, her eyebrows arching as she went along. Mom had big brown eyes, and when she registered surprise, it was pretty obvious.

"Steve, you want all *that* for one Christmas?"

I was a little startled by her reaction. It didn't seem like all that much to me. A few train accessories, some model planes to build, a selection of space toys, a miniature soldier playset . . . well, I didn't usually get everything I asked for anyway, so it seemed safer to ask for too much than too little.

"That seems a bit excessive, bud."

A bit shamefaced, I began to prune the extensive list of requests. Mom hadn't even seen the Christmas decorations I was going to ask for to deck out the house. I leafed longingly through the colorful pages, somehow trying to capture for our own modest home the aura that the book created for the magical holiday season, festive and celebratory.

"Why don't you go out and play?" she suggested, gently prying the catalog from my hands. "We'll make sure Santa hears about your list. And maybe you can write to him."

It shouldn't have been too surprising that my mother felt an inclination to suppress my greedy impulses. Her own upbringing had been Spartan, if not impoverished. When her father walked out on her family, a fugitive from the Immigration and Naturalization Service (or whatever it was called back then), he was a victim of his own indiscretions, and she was in her early teens, the eldest of four children.

The next few months were spent in a Catholic orphanage, while her mother recovered from a "nervous breakdown," followed by years in the public housing projects in the East End of Pittsburgh until my grandmother finally met a man who had an interest in her and her young brood. When my sister or I left food uneaten—or worse yet, attempted to throw it away—Mom spoke to us of her meager subsistence in those trying years: cabbage soup, ketchup reconstituted by rinsing the near-empty bottle with water, small portions of rationed sugar and meat during World War II. Since we were often the beneficiaries of the generosity of our grandparents, it was difficult to imagine just how spare her life had been.

I went out the front door, marching sullenly down the hill, and knocked at Mark's door, with my Johnny Eagle guns cradled in my arms.

"Wanna play army?" I asked when he appeared at the door.

Mark looked quickly over his shoulder, then burst through the screen door like something terrible was about to happen. "Gangway!"

I stood aside and gawked as two of his sisters tore out of the door after him. As the sole male child in a family with five kids, Mark seemed to enjoy more than his share of mischief. As I watched over the railing of the terraza, I saw him clear the bottom of the staircase, barely evading the grasp of his oldest sister, affectionately called "Midnight" in their household. I don't know what her real name was—I'd never heard her called anything else. She didn't bother with Mark much, being of the age to indulge in rather adult activities. But when he earned her contempt, he had to make tracks. She was clearly the most fearsome of the four sisters.

I tried to fade into the porch furniture as the two girls grumpily ascended the steps, pronouncing some choice judgments on their brother. Midnight turned in my direction, with dark, flashing eyes. My own eyes were wide with fear; I held up my hand and gently waved. She shook her head spitefully, and then marched inside, the screen door slamming behind her. She was very pretty but used too much eye makeup for my taste. While I really didn't think she needed it, I wasn't going to speak up.

When the coast was clear, I ran down the steps and headed for the gullies. The biggest and deepest of the ravines was our mutual sanctuary, agreed upon as our secret rendezvous point. The interlacing trenches were deep enough to obscure our whereabouts from any observers in the surrounding housing units, and the sagebrush added to the mystique and secrecy. I scampered down from Mark's driveway into the base of the depression, dodging the stones, rusting cans, and broken branches that littered the bottom. Moving quickly, I turned into a side trench, a smaller tributary but nonetheless deep enough to hide two boys. Mark was there, grinning at me as I arrived.

"Wow was she mad! What'd you do?" I asked, catching my breath.

"I told my mom and dad she was smoking in her room."

That sounded like a pretty dangerous thing to reveal to a very strict father. "Why?"

"She called me a little twerp! I fixed her—my dad will get her good."

"Here," I said, handing him a rifle. "I'll give you two minutes to hide."

"Ambush?" he asked. It was pretty much the only game we could play with just the two of us.

"Yeah, ambush."

I began counting loudly, hiding my eyes. Mark's feet clawed at the sandy, dry soil, sending small pebbles to the bottom as he climbed out of the ravine. I called out the last few numbers and retreated quickly in the direction I'd come. I knew his tendencies and where I believed I would find him.

Circling round behind our starting point, I climbed out of the trenches and took up position in some of the sticky shrubbery. I then waited patiently for what I thought would be his fatally flawed plan to unfold before me. Sure enough, in a few seconds, I could hear him advancing stealthily through the gully, trying to come around behind the spot where he'd last seen me—but I'd anticipated the move.

Mark and I had seen plenty of war movies: *The Longest Day, The Devil's Brigade, Kelly's Heroes, The Battle of Britain, The Green Beret.* They were all films that made combat seem glorious and exciting. We reveled in the thrills, the intense action, the loud and colorful explosions, the Hollywood version of heraldry and glory. I averted my eyes sometimes in the theater and somehow failed to appreciate the impact made on human flesh by bullets, blasts, and shrapnel. Cutting an adversary down seemed no more than a game, one that could be played over and over again—and that's exactly what we did. Our adventures made us feel grand and heroic, at least when we prevailed. And the seclusion we experienced when we stalked each other in that maze of trenches gave us a sense of isolation we cherished.

At times, when I felt the weight of my world closing in on me, lamenting some situation or interaction that had gone awry, I headed down into the gullies to escape. Out of sight and probably out of mind, I could mope about without fear of discovery, meandering through the sandy ravines until I could pull things together again and repair my mood or stroke my wounded ego, always watching carefully for lizard activity. After a quiz that didn't go so well or a scolding from my mother, it helped to lose myself down there. Chasing a lizard or two through the arid landscape often helped.

Occasionally, when playing our games, Mark or I would run through a trench only to be greeted by a "rat-a-tat-tat" machine gun report from a side gully, an unhappy flank attack as one or the other of us maneuvered to gain the element of surprise. But the most sought-after, the most delectable of situations, was a complete surprise attack from the rear. I was convinced that I was about to enjoy one of those.

By this point, I had worked my way up behind the main ravine into which I was sure Mark would soon be appearing—he'd be expecting to find me down there, likely with my back turned, waiting to catch him from some other direction. As I sat quietly behind a small collection of fragrant shrubs, he came into view, moving as cautiously as possible. The devious smirk etched on his features was amusing to me, for I knew how misplaced it was. Without a clue as to my whereabouts, he peered intently ahead and glanced to either side, tiptoeing his way through the debris at the bottom of the trench, then slowly elevating his head over the rim. He looked carefully in the direction from which we both had come. I let him settle into his ambush position while I observed him, all the while gleefully anticipating the terror I was about to unleash. At last, I could stand it no longer. I held my tommy gun up and carefully took aim. Running to the edge of the gully as noiselessly as possible, I let loose.

"Brrrat-brratt!" I called out, with my best impression of an automatic weapon.

Mark turned, shot me a look of complete astonishment, and crumpled into a heap on the ground.

I howled, "Ha! I got ya!"

He stirred, slowly standing and shaking his head as he brushed the sandy soil off his pants. His winsome smile returned, spreading quickly across his tanned face.

"How? How did you get back there?"

"I circled around you as fast as I could when I was done counting. You just went too slow."

"I think I gotta get home for supper. Midnight is probably calmed down by now."

"Yeah, I hope so, for your sake." I nodded to him and we began walking back.

Looking around at the sandy gulches in which we'd been playing, I figured we were lucky to have a place so close to home where we could escape from angry sisters or the cares of the day.

Even so, his statement made me shudder. My own sister was threatening enough when she got into a mood. Mark's big sister was frankly dangerous. I wondered what he would encounter when he slunk back into the house.

Nine

We walked out of the gullies, shuffling our feet through the gravel of the driveway as we went. As we passed the high wall that bordered his driveway, I noticed something odd. There at the base of the wall, lying motionless, was a lizard. A big one. A greeney.

"Look!" I said, immediately excited. I froze and dropped my voice to a whisper.

He followed my stare and replied in a muted voice, "Wow. What's he doing down there?"

Such a big lizard would never allow itself to be approached so closely by two people, but he lay quite still as we came toward him. Something was wrong.

"Maybe he's dead?" Mark suggested under his breath.

We crept closer. The lizard cocked his head and watched us intensely as we approached, but he was completely at rest except for the shift in his gaze. Well, he certainly wasn't dead. I could see his sides moving in and out with his breathing.

"I don't think he can run, Mark," I whispered.

We were directly over him now, and he hadn't flinched except to turn his head even farther to peer up at us. The poor creature looked as though he was expecting to be killed, and I felt a deep pang of sorrow for him.

I bent down and reached for him. Even though I knew lizards of his size had no teeth, I was still somewhat suspicious that he could turn his head and strike at me with his mouth. Surprisingly, he remained perfectly still, not moving a muscle as I held him, not even a twitch of the long, tapered tail.

"Something really bad must have happened," Mark pronounced, with a combination of sympathy and morbid curiosity.

"But he doesn't look hurt," I protested. "His tail is still on, and I don't see any blood or anything." I inspected as closely as I dared.

His long, reptilian body looked perfectly intact. The source of his inability to move was a mystery. But it was clear that he was helpless, and that he needed us.

"What are we going to do with him? I mean, he can't just stay out here, can he?" Mark pronounced the question that was going through my mind.

We both looked toward the gullies with dread. There were feral cats and rumors of wild dogs and probably other fierce animals. In short order, he'd be discovered and likely devoured.

"Well, he's not gonna live if we put him in a bucket," I said sorrowfully. "We can't even keep the healthy ones alive. Probably the best thing for him is to stay right here on this wall, where he lives."

I looked up and down at the gray stones. "Hey, look, here's a perfect hole for him."

There was a chink in the mortar between two large stones at about our eye level.

"It's the right size," Mark agreed. "That was probably his house."

I turned to him, holding the lizard out in front of me.

"But if he can't move, how will he survive, even in his own hole? He can't chase bugs, he can't run down to collect food, he can't do anything!"

I frowned, my enthusiasm tempered by the quandary my friend presented.

"Well . . . what if *we* feed him? *We* can take care of him. Every day we'll bring him some dead crickets or some raw hamburger. Maybe they're not his favorites, but they can keep him alive."

Inspired, Mark looked around. "Let's put him just inside the hole. So we can see him and put the food down right in front of him."

The plan was beginning to sound more plausible by the minute. We suddenly thought ourselves virtuous and clever. The lizard was nearly completely paralyzed and probably was destined to die. But we figured that if we could provide the daily care he needed to survive, then maybe, just maybe, we could nurse him back to health. It was a long shot, and we appreciated that, but it would be worth the attempt.

I placed him gently in the hole we had selected for his convalescence, backing him in, the long looping tail curling around and initially refusing to enter.

"He's pretty high up," my friend offered. "I don't think anything is gonna climb up there to get him."

I nodded vigorously. Then I had an idea. "Maybe another lizard would watch over him? Protect him? We could bring down one of those brownies from my terraza."

"Umm. I don't think it works that way," Mark countered.

The smile had faded from his thin lips. We both knew this was grave. For some reason, we'd been entrusted with the well-being of a paralyzed lizard, and the responsibility was intimidating.

It was now evening, and the shadows were lengthening. I stepped back from the wall, looking up at the glow coming from the picture window of my house. My mother would soon be calling me in for supper; there was no time to gather food for our charge. His first night in the sanctuary in which we'd placed him would be a long and hungry one.

Reluctantly, I told Mark that I was going inside and that I'd see him the next day after school.

"Then we'll get some crickets or something to feed him. I think he'll be all right till then."

I was at eye level with the terrified creature and looked at him closely. His dark, shining eyes seemed to meet mine. I felt as though he trusted us, that he somehow knew we were his only hope to recover from whatever had befallen him. I fought the urge to stroke him. Calling out a goodnight to Mark, I turned and ran up the hill.

It was really getting dark by then, and the lights of all the housing units were coming on. I paused to look out over the stretch of gullies. It was a dark and foreboding landscape. We never went into the gullies at night. During the light of day, I felt a sort of satisfaction peering out over this little patch of wilderness, as though we ruled it. But at night, snakes, and tiger centipedes, and who knows what else were prowling about.

"Will you get in here?" My mother had her hands on her hips as I shuffled in from the terraza.

It was suppertime, and there was no competition from the television, so our family always ate together and discussed the events of the day. My father presided.

"So what did you do today, Tom?" he asked, buttering some bread.

"Well, we found a lizard down by Mark's house . . ."

"No," he said, grimacing, "I mean in school."

His priorities definitely did not coincide with my own.

"Well, we did multiplication. And SRA. I read a story about mosquitoes coming out of a well and causing disease in another country. And then we practiced our dancing for an assembly—we're doing the Irish jig. And we started some drawings of Spanish castles for our books. Mr. Walden says we're gonna publish all our work in a real book at the end of the year! Oh, and then we did our book reports."

"Wow. Big day." My father clearly enjoyed my enthusiastic recounting.

"I really like my teacher," I said, gulping down my milk. "He teaches us how to do everything. And guess what?"

"How could I possibly guess 'what'?" he responded sardonically. It was his stock answer to the question I never tired of posing.

"We're going to the Royal Palace on a field trip!"

My mother gave me a sympathetic look, and my father seemed as enthused as I was. My sister, ever the cynic at that age, had nothing good to say.

"We've been there three times—what's the big deal?"

She was right—it was hardly new territory. Palaces weren't my favorite thing, after all: room after room of tapestries, intricate plasterwork, golden decorations, chandeliers, and the occasional throne. It was pretty cool the first time you saw it, considering it was the historic home of kings and queens, but after that, it was a lot less exciting. I preferred castles, fortresses, towers, even cathedrals. And, of course, gardens, where lizards hung out. Still, this visit would be with my class . . . the whole day out of school.

"Well, at least we're not going to a sewage plant," I spat back at Kathy, whose recent class trip to a wastewater treatment facility had been less than exotic.

She made a face, and then dismissed me altogether. It was positively infuriating how she could engage me for her amusement and then simply withdraw, suggesting that I was too immature to enter into an argument or even a conversation with her.

"Enough," my mother pronounced. "Kathy, you get to your homework. Do you have any, bud?"

I shook my head and pondered what to do to entertain myself. It was too late to go calling on friends. I sat at the dining room table and began leafing through one of the encyclopedias my father had purchased for us two years prior. The brilliant blue books were a source of pride for our family; they'd come equipped with a massive two-volume version of Webster's dictionary. When my father brought them home, we'd gathered around the dining room table and stared at the matching set of regal books in admiration. This was a symbol, surely, of learning and erudition. We didn't see such things in many of the other housing units when we visited friends in Royal Oaks. My father had placed them in a location of ready access and great prominence, on a bookcase purchased just for that purpose, onto which they fit perfectly, without a bit of space to spare.

The encyclopedia was symbolic of my father's respect for knowledge, though he was not a highly educated man. Restless and perhaps a bit too unbridled for the regimented and moralistic upbringing he'd received in the rural Shenandoah Valley, he had escaped to the Air Force as soon as he'd graduated from high school. While he seemed to have genuine affection for his parents, and appreciation for the bucolic life he'd left behind, he also liked to dance, and go to parties, and drink beer, as well as a few other things that were simply not acceptable in the German Baptist

Brethren culture of Mayland, Virginia. My mother noted that the people thereabouts were "almost Mennonites," though that didn't mean a lot to me when I was young. While he had not pursued a college degree after high school, Dad used the time to take college classes the University of Maryland offered to GIs on military bases, and he was over halfway to his degree. He made it clear that he believed my sister and I were intelligent, and he expected our grades and schoolwork to reflect it. It was important to me, as I suppose it is for most children, to gain the acceptance and praise of my father. What I could not accomplish on the athletic field, I was determined to manifest in my studies.

It was while leafing through these magnificent encyclopedia volumes, soon after my father had purchased them, that I'd stumbled upon the human anatomy transparencies. These glossy, see-through pages were adorned with colorful renderings of the individual organ systems: cardiovascular, neurologic, gastrointestinal, muscular, skeletal. And I fell in love. I fell in love with the human form, with the array of structures beneath our skins, with the organs that comprised us. I knew then that I would pursue the training to become a physician. And the creatures we pursued in the gullies or occasionally fished out of puddles behind the school simply added to the mystique and excitement of understanding the varieties of life in all its forms.

My own medical experiences cultivated my budding interests as well. When I'd sustained my head injury a year before during the freak hide-and-seek collision, doctors determined that my skull had been fractured and I needed surgery in a hospital in Germany. While my parents were nearly overwhelmed with anxiety, I found the entire process fascinating. As the surgeon explained that a shift in the impact by a fraction of an inch would have probably cost me my life, my mother turned ashen. But I tried to imagine what the doctor *actually* meant. I couldn't wait to get home to look at my anatomy pages, to go over the skull and the brain and the blood vessels, so I could piece it all together. As a souvenir, I was permitted to keep the IV catheter and tubing they'd placed in my arm to administer the anesthesia, which I treasured for years thereafter.

"Maybe you'll want to be a radiologist," my father advised when I told him of my interest in medicine. "They look at X-rays and tell the surgeons where to operate or if you have a broken bone."

That sounded good to me—I liked the anatomy maps and skeletons.

"Or maybe internal medicine."

When I asked about that specialty, he told me that those physicians tried to control illness and disease by using medications rather than cutting into tissues, like a surgeon. I thought about giving patients lots of shots and wondered if that would be for me. I'd once broken free of several attendants who were holding me down to get a shot of penicillin in my leg, and ran around the room, screaming, until they wrestled me into submission. I didn't want to cause that kind of terror for other people.

If my father doubted my capabilities to achieve this lofty goal, he did not make this apparent to me, but he did issue a bit of a caution. "You understand, Tom, that you'll be blazing a new trail. Nobody on either side of our family has ever been to college before, let alone medical school."

That made me think of the drones we'd read about. Maybe I had a particular purpose in life, and maybe that was to be a doctor.

I wondered, could I really be the standard bearer for a new era of education for our family?

On that particular night, while I was thinking about the helpless lizard for which we'd tried to provide sanctuary, I couldn't concentrate on what I was reading, and I went to bed early. I wondered what had happened to him, what was in store for him, and how he felt inside. Was he frightened and lonely? Or did he simply look at his reptilian life through the prism of fulfillment and pain, anticipating the source of his next meal and avoiding anything that posed a threat? Was he steely and indifferent to everything around him? Why, I pondered, did such terrible things happen to creatures? And to people?

As children, the Catholic Church taught us to value life in all its forms. I was fortunate that I didn't know any people with severe diseases or deformities when I was a boy, but this lizard had suddenly been thrust into my life. Clearly, it was my duty, and Mark's, to care for him. I vowed that, so long as he lived on that wall, I'd be ready to provide his basic sustenance. Maybe I'd even carry him around for a change of scene so he wouldn't be overcome by boredom.

I slept fitfully that night, dreaming of injuries, of paralysis, of suffering and hopelessness. When dawn finally awakened me, I dressed hurriedly for school, but I didn't have the time to go to the wall to check on our convalescent lizard.

Ten

I found myself wondering about the helpless little reptile all morning. I figured we'd check on him in the afternoon, after school let out.

Mr. Walden read aloud to us in the classroom, as he did almost every day, from a long list of his favorite books. "OK, class . . . where did we leave off?"

He inclined his head and studied the book, *Charlie and the Chocolate Factory*, which had quickly become a favorite among us.

"Here we go . . . Violet has just eaten too many blueberries . . ."

Even though he required all of us to read a book each week and to write a report according to his specific format, it was a lot more fun to sit and simply listen to Mr. Walden. Varying the inflection in his voice, allowing his tone to mirror the action of the tale, and meeting our eager eyes every few moments, he walked energetically through the classroom while he read, engaging us with his careful recitation of the story.

But on this morning, as much as I enjoyed listening to the adventures of the reluctant hero and the girl who turned blue from her indulgences, my mind continually went back to the injured lizard. I had a sense of foreboding about how this episode would end.

Finishing the chapter, Mr. Walden closed the book with a snap and moved us on to the next activity.

"OK, get out your notebooks and show me some drawings. I want you to do your best renditions of your very favorite places in Spain—castles, palaces, windmills, bridges, landscapes—whatever you love. Once you color them in, we'll use them to partition the chapters in your book."

As we worked, he walked up and down the aisles, complimenting students, offering suggestions, and making creative recommendations. He seemed to know a lot about everything.

"Steven," he said, looking at me curiously as he passed by my desk on his ceaseless rounds through the classroom, "you seem out of sorts today. What's the matter?"

I briefly met his gaze, then looked down disconsolately at my picture, a rendering of a fortress in nearby Toledo. I shrugged. I didn't want to discuss the disabled lizard in front of the class. I doubted anyone else would understand. Thankfully, Mr. Walden, always tactful, seemed to comprehend my reluctance and let the matter drop, applying a warm pat on my shoulder.

When the school day was over, I hurried home, hoping to catch Mark as he got off the school bus. My feelings of dread had intensified as the day wore on, and I didn't want to go to that wall alone. I walked briskly up the path through the gullies and past the rock wall that separated our units, deliberately averting my eyes. Trotting up to my terraza, I dropped off my bookbag, anxiously eyeing the road at the end of our driveway as I waited for Mark's bus to arrive. I turned to look at the gullies.

The terrain that had looked so threatening by night was now spread out below me in the bright sunlight, an inviting, sandy landscape punctuated by fragrant sagebrush. I recognized that it was a haven for wildlife, a delicate web of creatures and plants that depended upon each other for sustenance. The dark images of slithery serpents and sharp-toothed creatures that had haunted me the night before as I peered out in the forlorn darkness quickly dissolved as I regarded this placid, sunbaked landscape in the warm afternoon.

As the bus pulled up, the squeaking of the brakes startled me out of my reverie. I watched as the riders got off, including my sister and Marie. Mark was the last to walk down the stairs, giving ground gently to everyone else. It was his way. After looking to both sides as he hopped off the bus, he crunched his way through the loose gravel.

"Mark!" I ran down the stairs from the terraza as fast as I could, figuring I could meet him halfway down the steep descent. My sister passed me on the steps, pulling her books close to her to avoid colliding with me.

"Sorry, Kath, gotta go!" I cried, moving past her.

Mark was keenly aware of my concerns. The two of us trotted down the driveway, turning to the left along the front of his unit, paralleling the long, gray wall. We approached the granite barrier, its intricacies by now well known to us, and searched for the hole in which we'd placed the paralyzed lizard.

"He's gone!" Mark said, astonished. "Maybe he got his strength back!"

I swallowed hard, looking at the base of the wall and the weeds growing along it. There, in the tall grass directly below the niche in which we'd placed him, was the carcass of the lizard. He was covered with tiny black ants, which had devoured his eyes and much of the soft tissue inside of his now open mouth, as though he'd struggled to take his last breath with his jaws widely ajar. His scales proved a formidable barrier to eating the rest of the carcass, but in time, I was sure the ants would have their way.

I bowed my head, and Mark followed my line of sight.

"Oh," he offered quietly.

I stooped and reverently picked up the body, flicking off the swarming ants. The pests had established a supply line to the body from their nearby nest to take maximum advantage of the food supply that had just been delivered to them. Hundreds of the tiny insects had formed a swarming column between the anthill and the lizard's carcass. We called them "ant trails." Angrily, I scuffed at the insects with my shoe, scattering them in all directions.

The body was cool and limp in my hands.

"Wow, look how tiny his bones are." Mark was as fascinated as I was.

We peered at it, and I was captivated by the complexity of the small creature. The exposure of the eye sockets and some of the surrounding bone on the skull, which the ants had accomplished in a matter of hours, revealed the underlying skeletal essence of the reptile. He was now devoid of his prior character, no longer a member of the clever family that we considered our quarry. Now he was simply defunct. The bony structure of the skull was amazingly intricate, the orbital sockets black and yawning. Small plates of bone were delicately interconnected at the sutures of the skull, more closely fit together than any jigsaw puzzle I'd ever seen. I could scarcely believe, looking at his inanimate body, that but a few hours before there had been a vital creature contained within, which had now, devoid of life, morphed into this decaying shell.

Despite the revulsion I felt as I held the defiled body, I was fascinated by this collection of tissues. How, I wondered, could this assembly of disparate parts possibly co-opt to form a living creature? I thought of the transparent overlays of human anatomy in our encyclopedia, and how the organ systems related to one another. The disruption of whatever miraculous force cobbled these components into a functioning whole filled me with despair. Not simply because he was a member of the lizard family, but because this marvelous, vibrant animal had simply ceased to exist. Surely, the earth still had a place for him, and his departure should count as more than a source of food for an anthill.

I wrinkled up my face, unsure what feelings to express. I really loved lizards, but I was now ten years old; it wouldn't do to start tearing up. Mark bit his lip, and his eyes met mine.

"We have to bury him somewhere," Mark finally commented.

"I guess so," was all I could muster.

I thought a bit about what to do with the body. "Don't you think the ants will just get him again, and keep tearing him apart?"

"I know," he said brightly. "Let's build him a burial house. Out of stone."

I was puzzled. "Why?"

"Well, it'll give us something to remember him, like a tribute. He loved rocks and walls—what better place to bury him? And we can get him up off the ground so hopefully the ants won't get to him!"

I was a little relieved by this suggestion. "Maybe," I said, "it's the best we can do for him now."

It seemed appropriate to create for him a haven in death that he could no longer enjoy in life.

We placed the lizard back on the wall, certain his carcass would be safe for a short time while we collected stones of sufficient size and shape to fashion his tomb. The site we thought best for his memorial was a little garden at the base of Mark's stairs, where his mother had planted marigolds and other flowers that were still blooming copiously in the autumn sunshine. Course by course, we laid the masonry for the miniature temple.

"Do you have something to cover it with? You know, a roof?"

Mark thought for a moment and walked over to his carport, where he found a pair of small boards we could use. Inside the small mausoleum, we created a shelf upon which to place the lizard's body, intent on keeping him above the soil to reduce the chance that he would quickly be devoured by insects.

With great solemnity, I picked him up and placed his carcass, as gently and respectfully as possible, upon the stone shelf inside the mausoleum; Mark laid the roof boards over the crypt and we turned away. I looked down.

"I guess I'll see you tomorrow," I commented, and we both shuffled home, little left to say.

Though we'd both been insulated from the death of loved ones in our lives, the loss of this lizard, placed in our charge, was a powerful reminder of the fragility of life. The death of an animal was deeply upsetting to me. I'd once gone hunting with my father, his brother, and some of my older cousins in the cornfields of western Virginia, near his hometown. When the first rabbit was flushed and the shotgun blasts led to a breakneck tumble and a spurting of blood followed a spastic dance of the back legs, I utterly lost control of my emotions. In front of that group of sportsmen, with tears rolling down my face, I was intensely ashamed, and I knew I had embarrassed my father.

When I trudged up the stairs and through the front door, Dad saw immediately that I was crestfallen.

"What's the matter, Tom?" he asked in a kindly tone.

I was reluctant to discuss the demise of our lizard. I was afraid he'd regard my reaction as silly. As a man who'd grown up on a farm, he was much less sensitive to the death or suffering of animals than I was.

"You look like you lost your last friend." He crossed his thin arms and looked at me expectantly.

He was sitting in a big chair in our living room, wearing his white T-shirt and plaid Bermuda shorts—the typical uniform for relaxation when he was at home. Like his father, Dad was a skinny man, but he had acquired a rather awkward pot belly that stuck out too far for his frame. His arms, folded in front of him, rested comfortably upon this round bulge as he watched me.

I hung my head, uncertain whether my concern was ill-founded or reflective of some better part of my nature. Perhaps my intolerance of suffering among animals corresponded to my reluctance to compete or show an aggressive side in sports. Some part of me realized that I was simply too sensitive by nature, and this was not the way of the world.

"Me and Mark found a greenie yesterday—a big one—lying on the ground by that wall in front of his house. It couldn't move," I explained, watching Dad's face for any sign of real interest. "At least not very much. We think he fell off the wall and maybe broke his back. He could only move his head."

I looked up again to judge his reaction. His pale blue eyes were thoughtful.

I continued. "So we found a hole in the wall where he could live. We put him in there and figured we could feed him and take care of him. We didn't think he could live in a bucket. When we got home from school today, we found him lying at the bottom of the wall again, dead. Covered with ants. They were eating him."

Dad was quiet for a moment, then he looked at me fondly. "Steve, animals die."

It was a simple statement, which he delivered with gravity and an air of sympathy.

"Lizards don't live very long—you've even lost some healthy ones after a couple of days in your bucket. But the real point is that you cared. You tried to help him, and if he was as bad off as you say, he could not have lived more than a day or so. It was actually merciful for that suffering animal to meet his end. You can't prolong the life of a wounded animal that is beyond repair just because it's painful for you to see it die. Don't you see that God takes wounded creatures—and people—every day? It's actually a blessing that they go back to their creator. Death is the end of their suffering. For every animal, and every person, that moment will come. In your way, you eased his suffering on his last day on earth— that's a fine thing to do."

I felt a bit of my self-worth returning. "We built a stone burial house for him in Mark's garden. And we put a shelf inside to keep him out of the dirt, so the ants won't get him. Then we put a cross on top. You know, to bless him."

"I'm sure Mark's parents will truly enjoy seeing that lizard's shrine in their garden every day as they go up and down the stairs." I couldn't quite tell if he was hiding a smirk. Dad could be subtle with his humor.

"Thanks, Dad," I said, relieved. "I have homework to do. But can you read to me later?"

He nodded and then turned back to his paper.

Eleven

Not all the walls holding the earth in place in Royal Oaks were vertical. Some of them lay over on the earth sort of diagonally, holding a long, dry slope in place. It was easy for us to climb over these sorts of walls. As with all collections of rocks, these were havens for lizards, and we perused the nearby ones frequently, carefully springing from stone to stone, top to bottom, making a sort of game out of it, as if the rocks were stepping stones poking out of a languid stream. Once in a while, we were rewarded when a lizard ran out from underfoot, scampering back to its hole; just seeing one of these long, green lizards was a thrill. But we rarely, if ever, caught them in such circumstances—they were too big and fast, and the odds were all in their favor, anyway.

One warm afternoon in October, Mark and I walked over to one such wall, not far from our own quarters, and began hopping atop the gray, chiseled stones.

"I can't wait for Hallowe'en!"

"Me neither. We need to figure out our plan." I liked to configure things well in advance. It seemed to make our adventures more fun.

The housing development at Royal Oaks was an especially thrilling place to go trick-or-treating: gangs of kids in costumes roamed the streets, traffic was minimal, and pretty much everyone gave out candy. Sobering stories of poisoned treats or razor blades in apples hadn't yet made their way into our midst, and there was a wonderful air of innocent frivolity throughout the whole community.

Springing onto an especially big rock, I announced my intention for the upcoming holiday. "I wanna be Death," I said, resolutely. I'd given this some thought, as I had been especially spooked by a grim-reaper type character in a movie we'd gone to see.

"Death?" Mark echoed, puzzled, carefully measuring his footsteps as he followed me.

"You know—a skeleton with a big black robe and all that kinda floating around and scaring everyone."

"Oh. That death. How're you gonna make the costume?"

My mind went wild with possibilities. I envisioned a lifelike skull face, skeleton hands, a huge dark cape with a hood that revealed only the most terrifying glimpses of Death's head within, and a long, threatening scythe. Where I would obtain all this, I hadn't the faintest notion. The silly skeleton masks I'd used in the past—crinkly plastic things held in place with a flimsy elastic strap—just wouldn't do.

"How 'bout you? What're you gonna be?" I asked, still fixated on the image in my mind.

"A skeleton, I guess," Mark answered without so much enthusiasm.

"What's wrong with that? I love skeletons!"

"Well, I wore that costume last year. My mom says the outfit is still perfectly good."

"We can put some blood on it or something," I mused. "We'll make it better. And anyway, nobody remembers what you were last year. Even if they did, how would they know it was you again? That's the great thing about costumes!"

I looked around as we danced along the jagged stones. There was a large cardboard cutout of a skeleton on the front door of one of the units that faced us, and a picture window not far away featured two small bony apparitions dancing with each other.

"Let's call this the skeleton wall!" Mark announced, and I cheerfully seconded his motion.

We were elated in the way little boys often are when they acknowledge some situation of mutual enthusiasm. Somehow, it all fit together—my Grim Reaper costume, Mark's bloody skeleton, and the bony observers looking down upon us from the surrounding houses. It was the perfect site to commiserate upon all things Hallowe'en-ish, and we would return many times after school, over the next few weeks, watching the sun go down and the leaves on the gnarled oaks turning brown, to frolic along those stones and to plan our outing.

One dark evening, we convinced Mike to come over and plot our adventures with us.

"This is the skeleton wall!"

"Cool," Mike observed, taking stock of the decorations around us.

"Me and Mark are gonna be skeletons for trick-or-treat! Well, I'm dressing up as Death, but that's like a skeleton. How about you? Do you want to be a skeleton too? That'd be so neat—all of us with skulls and bones!"

He wasn't convinced. "I want to be a vampire," he said, ignoring my suggestion.

"Well," Mark chimed in as he balanced on a particularly rounded stone, "that could still be good. Skeletons and vampires are both pretty scary!"

I assented, and we affirmed our plans that very evening.

When we met to discuss our plans for Hallowe'en over the next week, our imaginations conjured up illustrious scenes of doom, terror, and fright as more cardboard witches and ghosts were taped to windows as the gloomy evenings fell upon us ever-earlier. We watched as our shadows lengthened over the rocky crust of the skeleton wall and the hollows of the stones themselves began to appear as ghastly as the vacant eye sockets of the bony spooks we sought to emulate. At school, the excitement surrounding the holiday was amplified by the songs we sang, the pictures we drew, the chilling stories our teachers read to us. That we were surrounded by people in a country with no interest in or understanding of All Hallow's Eve meant little to us, and in fact may have intensified our thrills.

On the day of Hallowe'en, Mike and I walked home together after the entire elementary school had gathered for an assembly with music and singing. The lyrics of one song echoed within my mind.

"Trick or treat tonight! How's that song go again?"

"Something about dead leaves and witches in the sky," I said before launching into the song as boisterously as I could. That tune stirred within us fearful visions, and we repeated it again and again as we made our way back up through the gullies.

Central Spain didn't offer much of an autumn, but as winter approached, a few trees dropped lifeless brown leaves that collected at their bases and rattled in the warm breezes like ancient, brittle bones. Waiting anxiously for our friend, we met Mark after he got off the bus.

"OK, we've got about an hour for supper."

"Right," Mark agreed. "Let's eat and get our costumes on and then meet over at the skeleton wall. Perfect place to start our haunting!"

"And to sort our candy when we're all done." I couldn't stop thinking about chocolate bars, lollipops, and candy corn—enough to last till Thanksgiving, if we were careful.

In short order, we stole over in our costumes as the evening shadows fell.

"That's pretty scary," Mark observed, looking over my rendition of the Grim Reaper.

Mike, made up as a vampire, complete with fangs, a cape, and blood trickling from the corners of his mouth, nodded energetically.

"You look just like Barnabas Collins," I told him. I didn't really know who that was, but we liked to play a board game called Dark Shadows, and he looked like the title character, a vampire who adorned the front of the box.

Mike smiled overtop his artificial fangs. "That's exactly what I was trying for," he said with satisfaction.

I was a little envious that Mike always seemed so confident, able to accomplish what he set out to do, whereas I approached the challenges of life with a measure of self-effacement and doubt.

"What do you think of my scythe?" I asked, brandishing a broomstick with a rather flimsy scabbard, taken from a small toy sword, affixed to one end.

Even through their disguises, I could see that they looked doubtful.

"Scythe," I urged them. "You know, that long, curved cutting thing the Grim Reaper carries around? My dad has a real one he uses to cut weeds with. He wouldn't let me use it. "

Mike was amazed. "Why not? That would be so neat!"

"Well, he said it's too dangerous out here in the dark," I countered a bit defensively.

No one objected to that explanation, so we turned our attention to other matters. Standing in the gathering dusk on top of the wall, we planned our route.

"First, let's go down to the lower streets, by TC's house," I suggested.

Mark and Mike nodded, and it struck me that it would be funny to see a group of spooks and skeletons piecing together a plan to collect candy.

"Then, we'll come back up here—we'll scare the neighbors!"

We were perhaps a little too confident in our costumes and how frightful we looked.

"Yeah, and then come over here to the wall, then stop at all these places," Mark indicated the homes surrounding us, "and then eat as much candy as we can before we have to go home."

We would celebrate by gorging on our favorite candies and discussing the most terrifying sights of the evening. A waxy quarter moon rose and oversaw our council, though it was hidden periodically by thin, streaky violet clouds.

We made our way into the darkness, down a grade and around the bend, toward the house of my sister's friend, Dina. She lived close to the prestigious neighborhood that abutted Royal Oaks, called La Moraleja, where John Wayne supposedly owned a home. We were forbidden to trespass in that area, as all the houses were large and gated, and the Guardia Civil were on active patrol.

At Dina's house, we found a creepy cemetery occupying the front yard, gently backlit by a green spotlight that threw crazy shadows. A knot of young trick-or-treaters gathered on the sidewalk just outside the lawn, apparently afraid to encroach any farther on the hallowed ground.

"Hah. Real scary," Mike snickered, leading us closer.

We scowled at their soft, furry little animal costumes, as well as the occasional unimpressive spook in their midst, and we were not surprised at their timidity. As we arrived, hooting and howling, they dispersed, uncertain whether the path through the graveyard or the recently arrived ghouls were more intimidating. It was a satisfying moment, a recognition of the fear we were certain we engendered in the hearts of the average Hallowe'en ghost or witch.

"Well, this looks pretty scary," I admitted to my friends as we took stock of the situation.

The general din of Hallowe'en echoed throughout the neighborhood: screams of fright, calls for candy, maniacal laughter receding into the darkness. Mike strode down the path, unfazed.

"Well," he scoffed, "a lot of kids already have a head start. It's time to get some candy."

Mark and I followed, looking around nervously.

"What's that?" Mark's voice quivered, just a bit.

As we approached the carport, I saw, to my utter astonishment, a life-sized casket surrounded by tall, flickering candles that cast a dim light on the oblong box. And that was all. There was no one else about, nor a sound to disturb the scene. Mike slowed and we caught up, all of us eyeing the coffin nervously. There was a sidewalk leading to the front door, but it was dark and uninviting. The funereal scene was clearly where we were meant to go for our trick-or-treat satisfaction.

"Maybe there's a candy bowl," I said hopefully, looking awkwardly through the holes in my mask.

We stood for a moment, unsure what to do. Then, a second later, the lid of the coffin swung open, and a creature, wrapped in bloody bandages, sat up, clawed fingers outstretched.

"Aaagh!" it wailed, reaching as though intending to bring us into its clutches.

Collectively, the three of us left the surface of the earth for several seconds, then recoiled in terror as we landed, gasping in turn.

"Happy Hallowe'en!" the specter called, and I recognized the voice of Dina's father, whom I'd met at some point when Kathy and I had visited.

We collected ourselves and reluctantly approached the casket.

"Wow, that was so spooky!" Mike laughed nervously.

SweeTARTS were handed out to each of us—the really big kind you could suck on for hours. They were a fitting reward for what we'd been subjected to. Shaking off our startled reactions, we thanked Dina's father and fled through the ghastly graveyard and headed down the road.

There followed a long string of more conventional knocks on the door, followed by displays of our costumes in the porch lights, and, all too often, a request for an explanation of exactly what *I* was supposed to represent.

"I thought this was pretty obvious," I said after a few such instances.

"I think it's that scythe-thing. It's just not realistic," said Mark, acknowledging what I knew was at least part of my problem.

"Yeah. Plus, that hood covers up your mask. You look like Little Black Riding Hood!" Mike hooted.

As if I needed the sarcasm.

At least Mrs. Reimolds was impressed. And, fortunately for me, she had received advance notice of my costume, so she had no trouble recognizing what I purported to be.

"Very scary," she confirmed, offering the same to my partners as she plumped up our candy bags with Hershey bars.

It was on the return route, moving back up the grade on the other side of the road, keeping a respectful distance from the dim cemetery scene, that we met our comeuppance.

It was dark enough that shadows played tricks with our eyes, and, since we were wearing masks, our visual fields were a bit compromised.

"What's that?" Mark slowed, peering into the darkness.

As we walked up the grade, we could just make out, jaunting towards us with enormous strides, a very tall man in a black suit, perhaps a tuxedo with tails.

"I can't tell . . . He's awfully tall . . . It's pretty weird." I felt a chill as I watched him.

He was alone in the darkness as he sauntered down the street. What was astonishing was not so much his extraordinary thinness, his apparent height, or his ungainly gait, but that he appeared to have . . . no head. And the closer he came, the clearer this became to us, shadows or no shadows, masks or no masks. Our little party came to a standstill, perhaps out of respect, perhaps out of paralyzing fear, until he strode between us, close enough to touch, tall enough to dwarf each of us.

We were frozen with fear. And at that moment, when he might have reached out and grabbed any one of us, he let out an ear-splitting laugh that boomed through the darkness. From what part of his body this bone-chilling sound was emitted, I don't know! Could a headless man laugh?

"Trick or treat, my little friends!" the voice screeched.

Then, most macabre of all, I realized he was carrying his head in his hands, and the laughter and words sounded as though they had emanated from the contorted mouth of this detached sphere.

This was beyond the usual Hallowe'en fright. We scattered in abject terror, crossing the road, chocolate bars and popcorn balls bouncing out of our bags and onto the asphalt that we pounded with our racing feet.

"Run! Run!"

But Mike needn't have told us what to do.

The three of us made for the other side, sprinting for the familiar, reassuring neighborhood of the skeleton wall. I was usually the fastest among us, but not that night. The lead changed hands repeatedly until we finally arrived, panting and trembling from fright, excitement, and adrenaline.

Collapsing upon the ground, we tossed our candy bags onto the wall and began to laugh, almost hysterically.

"Was that real?"

"Couldn't be real . . . could it?"

"I think I saw the eyes moving in his head!"

A more realistic and frightening costume we could not have imagined. Royal Oaks was small enough, and we were central enough in the housing complex as we sat on our wall, that we could trace the route of this ghoul as he strutted around the neighborhood, evidenced by the shrieks of fear and surprise that erupted from each group of costumed revelers he encountered.

Meekly, we completed our rounds, knocking on the doors of the units that faced the wall we had claimed as our own. Finally, with bags once again filled to overflowing, we made for home. The curfew hour was upon us, and all around we saw spooks, witches, and goblins shuffling back to their units.

"Man," Mike giggled, "that was the best."

"Yeah, the best," I acknowledged.

It was a bittersweet moment. As I retraced the evening's adventures in my mind, I realized that Mark and I, both slated to leave the following summer, would not spend any more Hallowe'ens in Royal Oaks. And we had to consider that, given our ages, we might never go trick-or-treating again.

Twelve

"Is that them?"

Kathy pointed excitedly toward a throng of people arriving as we stood in a crowd waiting at Barajas Airport outside Madrid. The amiable chatter of friends and relatives surrounded us as they rushed at one another, hugging and kissing enthusiastically, as a jumbo jet discharged its passengers.

I felt a little thrill. It *was* them. "Hey, Gram! Hey, Gramps!"

It had been almost three years since I'd seen any of my extended family. I couldn't contain myself and rushed over to throw my arms around my grandparents, who'd just flown over from the United States. My grandparents were the first family visitors to come to Spain, and we were thrilled at the prospect. My mother, sister, and I had lived with them for a year in their three-story house while my father was in Vietnam. Number 1 Wynoka Street was on a brick street in Carrick, a neighborhood in the south of Pittsburgh. They shared the house with my uncle, aunt, and cousin Rick, who was a good friend to me. Their kindness to us, their affable natures, and their willingness to share everything they possessed had been a tremendous comfort in helping me cope with my father's long-term absence.

Their "big yellow house on the hill" constantly bustled with activity. The refrigerator was always full of good things to eat, and my grandfather regularly appropriated fresh produce from the boxcars he unloaded at the fruit auction down in the strip district. Both of my grandparents were corpulent and jolly. Gramps's sense of humor was legendary, at least among those who knew him. He had a terrible penchant for repeating jokes and funny phrases. And he was an unapologetic bigot, but his joviality and his willingness to poke fun at himself made this tolerable and even humorous. My grandmother tolerated his antics, sometimes with frustration but typically with just a bit of good-natured scolding. The two of them reveled in the company of their grandchildren, and they never stopped thinking about ways to amuse and treat us.

They looked a little sleepy, but both were as joyful as we were for the reunion. Asked how things were back home, Gramps was only too happy to fill us in.

"You know your grandmother—she loves a party. She drags me and Ricky around to parades, parish carnivals in the schoolyards, and every Polish festival that comes up. It's nonstop. I drive her all over Pittsburgh!"

Like her daughter, Gram had big brown eyes and was very practiced at rolling them to counter Gramps's exaggeration.

Kathy and I routinely spent time in Pittsburgh during the summers. My grandmother and aunt ensured that there was always plenty for us to do: trips to the amusement park at Kennywood, boat rides on the river, and excursions to the zoo and other local parks. When the weather turned dreary, we were escorted to the Carnegie Museum to see the dinosaurs, the Buhl Planetarium, or the neighborhood movie houses. In between, we visited shopping malls and hobby shops or just tagged along on errands. There was always something to do in Pittsburgh. Our lives before and after our visits to their house were staid by comparison.

My two delightful grandparents seemed to bring their verve with them wherever they went—most importantly, they brought their joy and energy to our house whenever they visited. There were always gifts, stories about how our cousins were doing, and plenty of food. The city offered delectable fare that we did not experience in the other places we lived: fancy cold cuts and hard dinner rolls with poppy seeds, freshly baked goods, and unusual cuts of meat like "city chicken," which I learned was breaded pork on a stick and not chicken at all. Of course, there were all sorts of produce, including many things we could not buy where we lived, including kiwi fruit, ripe cherries in big crates, and tangy strawberries shipped in from California long after our growing season had passed.

"You don't remember," my mother told me, "but when your dad was a staff sergeant, we barely scraped by. Paying the bills was a struggle sometimes. So when your grandma and Chuck came to visit us in Cumberland, they would bring a whole trunk-load of food, and of course some treats for you kids. That went a long way toward easing our monthly grocery bill. They were really good to us."

"Now it's our turn to treat them!" Dad seemed pleased at the prospect.

My father was fond of his parents-in-law, referring to Gramps as "Pittsburgh Party Charlie" and my grandmother as "Ma Pitt." My mother called them "Mum and Chuck," as Gramps was actually her stepfather. When my grandfather began courting Gram, he was not a young man, and he was not prepared to deal with four unruly children who had been fatherless for some years. He proved an unholy terror for the children when he first married into the family, and there was turmoil in the house. Stories abounded of his temper tantrums, including once when he cut the power cord to the newly acquired television set, because the volume was set too loud. My mother, the eldest of the children, fled the home at her earliest opportunity, joining the Air Force when she was only seventeen years old.

"I had to get out," she once confided to Kathy and me. "I couldn't take Chuck's temper. Basic training in the Air Force was easier than dealing with him. And when they asked us who liked to fly, I put my hand up." Here, she always laughed. "I had never flown in my life, except for my trip down there, but it sounded adventurous. And I became a stewardess in the Military Airlift Transport Service."

The Air Force did not permit a husband and wife to be on active duty in those days, so she had to leave her career soon after they became engaged. But she was proud of her service and her adventurous spirit.

I suppose her short stint on active duty made life as a dependent wife much more tolerable.

Though she had fled her home when my grandfather had arrived all those years ago, my mother admitted that he had become a different man as a grandfather. What Gramps had failed to provide in love and tenderness to his step-kids, he more than made up for with his grandchildren. Indulgent to a fault, he was beloved by all of us, endlessly kind and attentive. And always witty.

"Your grandfather may not have made it past the eighth grade in school, but he has a lot of street smarts. And he can make a joke out of most anything." Dad smiled when he confided this to me.

And with his bluster and affable nature, even the things Gramps said that weren't outright funny were amusing. "I wish I could've slept on the plane, but your grandmother was snoring loud enough to keep all the other passengers awake!"

They were exhausted but characteristically jocular. It was satisfying to feel their arms around me. Kathy was enthusiastic about their visit as well, but a bit less affectionate. It seemed it was no longer proper at her age to rush headlong into a crowd and start hugging her grandparents. Still, it was a joyous reunion.

"Now, let's have some fun," Gramps said, putting his arm around us both after shaking my father's hand vigorously. "When do we eat?" he asked with a grin.

"Be quiet. We're not here ten minutes and you're looking for food," my grandmother chided.

She served as his wife, his servant, and his parent. Gram often scolded, but her nature was such that everyone knew it was mostly pretense. We typically just bowed our heads apologetically until she spoke her piece and became her warm, affectionate self again.

"Steverino," my grandmother began, sizing me up. "What have they been feeding you over here? You're skinnier now than when you left Pittsburgh!"

I was not a very substantial boy, and I had heard my share of complaints about my size from many of my relatives, especially on my mother's side. They were generally large people, while I'd had the misfortune to inherit my habitus from my father's side of the gene pool; his relatives tended to be wiry and slight.

"Don't worry, your grandmother will be here for two weeks—she'll help your mom put a few pounds on your little body!" My grandfather clearly envisioned eating robustly while my grandmother cooked alongside my mom during the visit, and I felt their love in these food offerings. I'd certainly try to do my part. My stature probably played a role in my shyness among people and my hesitation on the baseball diamond, but I figured I'd fill out as I aged, and that these problems would simply resolve.

It felt natural to have them in our quarters, even though the apartment was small. The two of them stayed in Kathy's room, and she had to sleep on a cot in mine, which produced a degree of indignation she took no pains to hide. As if it were some treat to have her in my space!

After supper, we all sat around the table and caught up on each other's lives in Spain. Gramps was fascinated as we described the things we'd seen and done. He was intensely proud of his Italian heritage and never tired of reminding us that while Christopher Columbus had sailed to America from Spain, he was actually an Italian explorer. Gramps's last name was Samarco, but it had reportedly derived from San Marco, which sounded Spanish enough. During his visit, he frequently brandished this moniker in our broken conversations with tradespeople or shopkeepers, trying to imply that he had ancestors in Spain.

"Time for slides!"

As with everyone who came to visit us, Gram and Gramps were subjected to the collection of photos my father had taken while we traveled across the Spanish countryside, in the form of a slide show. With popcorn and enthusiastic narration, it was a pleasant way to spend the evening and a good substitute for television, which was all in Spanish, anyway.

"What's that?" Gram asked, looking at a picture of the vast cathedral in Sevilla, where I'd raced around with TC just a few months before.

"That's where Columbus is buried."

"A truly great Italian." Gramps never missed the opportunity to praise the luminaries from the country of his ancestors.

"And that?"

"Those are the Roman ruins in Cordoba—it was once a grand amphitheater. They're still digging it out."

"You see? The Romans were everywhere," Gramps said. "They conquered the whole world!"

"Chuck, have some more popcorn," Mom advised. He didn't talk as much when his mouth was full. There were still a lot of slides to go.

The next day was a Saturday, so my mother packed a picnic and we headed for a local town that was renowned for its medieval architecture. Segovia had once been the site of a Roman settlement. Perhaps its greatest claim to fame was the two-thousand-year-old, hundred-foot-high aqueduct that had carried water into the town. This remarkable structure was still standing, and it remained in use, though it moved the water in pipes rather than open troughs. The aqueduct was said to be one of the finest examples of an intact Roman structure in the world.

"Helen, check this!" Gramps announced as we drove into the town and passed directly under the soaring arches of the aqueduct. "Stevie, what'd I tell you. Those Italians were the greatest builders in history. Thousands of years later, their roads and bridges are still standing." His pride was almost palpable as he made this announcement. "And not just here—all over Europe!" he added enthusiastically.

My grandmother politely ignored him.

"Helen, look at the castle!" he roared.

In the ancient Spanish towns we visited, there were usually two types of historic attractions—a cathedral and some sort of castle, fortress, or palace. Segovia was even more interesting, as it offered the superb aqueduct as well as the other usual attractions. The Alcázar, which had been constructed to protect the town, was amazing to behold. The castle stood out on the spur of a high ridge above a valley, like the prow of a mighty ship, turrets towering above the thick stone walls. These were topped by tall, conical roofs. In the center of the fortress was a large rectangular tower, crowned by battlements, which presided over the interior of the castle grounds.

"Look, Gramps!" I pointed to the top of the tower, where we could just make out tiny figures of people peering over the battlements.

"That's quite a fort. I don't know what army could hope to attack it!" he said. "That must be a real view from up there."

Given its carefully selected geography, massive size, and multiple layers of defense, the Alcázar appeared to be impregnable.

We jumped out of the car and approached the massive cathedral, with spires, towers, and buttresses soaring above us. We never failed to visit these impressive catholic landmarks for an appreciation of their architecture, for a profound sense of the piety that peasants must have felt centuries before as they shuffled in for Mass, and for a look at the stunning collection of priceless artifacts each parish had sequestered. Of course, we also made time for a moment of silent prayer.

My grandmother, who'd spent her life in America among Polish immigrants, was no stranger to outsize Catholic churches, which had sprung up in many neighborhoods and towns in Western Pennsylvania. Some of these could have been deemed cathedrals in their own right. Still, she was awe-struck by the towering sanctuary of the cathedral in Segovia, with its vaulted chambers, numerous altars, and splendid stained-glass windows. As we entered, the prayerful hush that dominated within quickly enveloped us. Far to the front, a priest's voice droned, quietly reciting the liturgy for a small group of townspeople at a side altar.

Reflexively, Gram dipped a finger in the holy water and crossed herself. We quickly followed suit.

A simple woman, my grandmother was devoutly religious. Many adversities had shadowed her life, but she never wavered in her steadfast belief in God and Catholicism, or in her enthusiastic promotion of the faith among her family members.

My mother stood a few steps away and looked at me expectantly. She clearly wanted me to leave Gram alone.

"Give her a moment," she whispered.

I shrugged. I was content to let my beloved grandmother worship in the manner she wished.

"Gram isn't allowed to take communion, so it's important for her to pray when she enters a church. She just needs to be left on her own for a few minutes."

"Why can't she take communion?"

I'd seen Gram in church, bowing her head while kneeling on her arthritic knees in the pew, as others around her, no more pious than she, joined the line to receive the host.

"Your grandfather—your real grandfather—left her when we were little. And she raised us on her own, with help from the parish, for almost ten years. Till she met Chuck. When she asked the Church for an annulment so she could marry him, the parish wanted five hundred dollars. They couldn't afford it, not back then. So she had to get married outside the Church. That means she can never take communion."

To me, that series of events seemed supremely unfair, but I was not well acquainted with the laws that governed the Roman Catholic Church.

Later in my life, when my own faith had simply evaporated during a decade of smug self-righteousness, I nonetheless continued to harbor great respect for the devotion shown by both my mother and my grandmother, and their unwavering commitment to their beliefs. Neither of them was a great reader or reciter of the scriptures, preferring, in the Catholic tradition, to have an interpretation of the Word provided to them by the priest.

I could sense my mother's bitterness as she described this course of events. I'd previously heard her express distaste and frustration with the Church. But criticism never translated into avoidance of Mass or exploration of other denominations. After all, as she once told me, "an angry Catholic is still a Catholic."

Even though we were not there for Mass, I could see an immediate change in my grandmother's demeanor inside the cathedral. She was in the House of God. Her head was bowed low, while her dark eyes had a distant intensity. I supposed she was praying as she admired the inside of the cathedral. We shuffled silently through the main aisles and moved into a short hallway leading to the treasury. Most Spanish churches, even the small ones, had a fine collection of religious implements collected over the centuries, gold and silver cups and other items, often encrusted with precious stones. They were fun to look at, if only to imagine their worth, but this quickly became boring for me. I did not, in my immaturity, appreciate the pride an individual parish would have for its collection of fine antiquities, nor how each of these items represented the work and worth of the community as a whole. It was not apparent to me then that these implements had been purchased with the labor, taxes, and contributions of the townspeople.

As we gazed upon the gold and silver chalices and crucifixes, my grandfather, whose two major religious themes were eating and sleeping, just had to make a crack. "It's a wonder the Pope hasn't come by to collect all this stuff," he muttered sarcastically.

"Shut up, Chuck," Gram hissed. She tolerated his jovial and sardonic nature almost all the time, ignoring his good-natured ribbing. But not there. Not in church.

I'd been ushered through the appropriate sacraments at that point in my life: baptism, communion, reconciliation, and even confirmation. Four down, three to go, I figured. And it was pretty easy to be pious, obedient, and prayerful, especially when I needed something. But the great stresses of life had not yet begun to savage me as they had my grandmother and my mother. I had much to learn, and the tests of my faith were yet in the future.

We blessed ourselves again with holy water, indulged in the appropriate gestures, and made our way into the bright sunshine. Having visited the great cathedral, we were anxious to shop for souvenirs and tour the towering Alcazar castle.

Thirteen

Segovia was bathed in warm autumn sunlight, humming with the excitement of visitors who had come to admire its centuries-old edifices. Innumerable souvenir shops lined the streets, most of them no more than tiny storefronts, doors wide open, a variety of keepsakes and curios tumbling out onto the sidewalks in front of them. The main street teemed with tourists ducking in and out of the shops, haggling enthusiastically for their choice memorabilia.

Shuffling his portly frame along the cobblestone walkway, my grandfather espied an antique broadsword that looked at once intimidating and intricate. Its handle was stout, its blade impressively shiny, with fanciful script inlaid along its surface.

"Hey, Helen," he called to my grandmother, who was sidewalk-shopping with my mother a few stores back, "check this. This is the real McCoy!"

He held the sword up in a defensive posture in defiance of an imaginary enemy. I was amused. But with his short stature and corpulent frame, he looked much less like the heroic figure of the legendary El Cid than he did Sancho Panza, the rotund, comical sidekick of Don Quixote.

The storekeeper regarded us and walked out eagerly. He realized we spoke English and were probably from the U.S. His complexion was darker than most men we met in central Spain, and he had a small, bent frame.

"How much?" my grandfather asked.

"Cuanto es?" I translated, trying to be helpful.

"Mil pesetas," the owner said proudly, holding up the sheath that belonged to the sword.

"That's a thousand pesetas, Gramps," I said seriously. At that time, that was a lot of money for an old sword in Spain.

"Hmmm. Ask him if he'll take five hundred," Gramps countered, looking away as if he'd lost interest. A master of subtlety, he turned and winked at me. "He's just starting high. I'll get him down."

"No. Mil pesetas," the man said firmly, turning up his nose and refusing to make eye contact.

The two men faced away from each other and continued to barter, with me as the intermediary. My father approached, watching with interest.

"Ask him about six hundred" was the next request.

I translated in turn. "Seiscientos pesetas?"

The man acted outraged, as though the request was a personal attack. But he wasn't going back into the store. My grandfather turned to me again, suggestively raising his eyebrows. His thick glasses magnified his eyes, and he appeared very confident.

"OK, OK. Six hundred fifty. I can't go higher."

"Seiscientos y cincuenta pesetas," I said. "No mas."

"No mas? No mas?" The man became animated, holding his hands up in the air.

He then grabbed the sword and spoke so fast that I could not begin to understand, lovingly moving his fingers across the blade, pointing out the unusual writing, and saying something about an ancient king during whose reign the piece was apparently forged.

At this point, my grandfather was exasperated. Either he was genuinely frustrated that he wasn't getting his way, or he was doing a fine job of acting.

"I have to go. I can't pay any more than that."

"Gracias," I offered to the store owner. "Adios."

Gramps made a big show of adjusting his hat, taking one last look at the sword, and walking defiantly away. I nodded to the man and followed Gramps, who walked slowly to the storefront next door, where he pretended to be interested in a table of trinkets. He glanced back briefly as the vendor made an equally big show of re-shelving the sword in its place.

I wanted Gramps to have that sword.

"I bet he sells it for seven hundred," I whispered as I caught up.

"Seven hundred?" he asked me in a louder voice.

"Setecientos?" asked the tradesman, glancing toward us. Apparently, he knew some English.

Suddenly, the game was back on. The man picked up the sword and held it out. My grandfather inclined his head and smiled.

"You look great with that sword, Gramps."

He was clearly satisfied with himself as he pulled out the peseta notes and handed them over.

In keeping with the pretense each had displayed during the transaction, the man behind the counter looked hurt, as if he'd been taken advantage of. I suspected he was secretly pleased but wanted to let my grandfather think he'd gained the upper hand. Everybody seemed to win, and I was gratified that I had helped the deal go down.

Gramps stashed his "real McCoy" in our car, and we headed to the Alcázar. He and I walked across a drawbridge that extended over a deep, threatening moat. There was a craggy, rock-filled trough in front of a ravine that must have been a hundred feet deep, as if this castle, perched as it was on the heights above the town, was not already ideally situated for the defense of the people. I was mesmerized by the view from the drawbridge, peering meekly over the railing.

"C'mon, bud," my mom said, coaxing me along. She didn't have the same appreciation for such things as I did.

Gramps strutted into the castle, passing under the main gate as though he belonged there. I was right beside him, telling him some of the things I'd learned about the Alcázar in my prior visits. For one thing, I explained, the castle had been one of the models for Sleeping Beauty's castle in Disneyland when that theme park was constructed decades earlier. And, we were once told during a tour, a servant who was caring for the royal couple's daughter came too close to one of the windows, and, in a frantic moment, lost control of the moving child, who suddenly fell over the ledge and hundreds of feet to the rocks below. Out of sheer terror, the young woman then leapt to her death out of the same window. Gramps seemed impressed.

We gathered with a small group of tourists awaiting a guide to take us through the fortress.

"Gramps, let's go up to the top of the tower!" I urged, looking up at the top of the massive square structure in the middle of the courtyard. It loomed impressively over the approach to the fortress.

He looked a bit anxious at this suggestion but assured me we could go up after the tour.

Much to my grandmother's embarrassment, Gramps managed to put himself at the center of attention throughout the tour. He had a joke prepared for every situation—kings, castles, thrones, knights, swords, ladies-in-waiting. And if he didn't have a pre-arranged one, he made up some pun or play on words on the fly.

"Hey, do you mind stepping a little to the side?" he asked one couple as we stood in a semicircle in the armory, admiring the suits of armor. "I'm a little on the short side . . . At work, they call me a 'mini-Guinea,'" he reported with a loud, amused snort.

Just a few moments later, as we shuffled into the throne room, I heard him guffawing as he made his way through one of his standard jokes, and, while reporting the punch line, he held his hand up to his ear as he impersonated an elderly nun: "Father who?"

It was off color, but a soft chortle sifted through the crowd.

Despite his educational limitations, Gramps had a sharp mind. I was continually amazed at how quickly he could come up with a snappy line. Our guide, a meek but kindly Spanish lady, thin of build with dark ringlets of hair, was overshadowed by his brassy exuberance, but she was polite and tolerant. By the end of the tour, she would pause after each of her talking points to allow my grandfather to add his own humorous perspective. Had I been older, I might have found this rude, but he had a marvelous effect on the others and was chatting cheerfully with the entire group as if they were old friends by the end of the tour.

"You should come to Pittsburgh. We can sit on my front porch, drink some Iron City, and play pinochle," he assured one man and his wife, who were visiting from New Jersey.

"Tell 'em, Jerry. The fun never ends at my house," Gramps said. "We got two families, two grandchildren, two kitchens, a dog, and a never-ending stream of visitors. I call it the House that Jack Built."

My father pressed a hundred-peseta note into the guide's hand, giving her an appreciative look.

"Gramps, let's go up!" I called, and he followed me to the base of the tower.

He was a vigorous, hard-working man but not athletic. In truth, he was pretty obese. Climbing the ancient stairs as fast as I could, I frequently had to go back down a few steps to urge him on. I nearly had to tug him up the last few flights of stairs. He was huffing, puffing, and red in the face as we reached the top, but as enthusiastic as ever. Until I took him to the edge. There was a thick, relatively high wall around the flat top of the tower, with low cut-outs to allow whatever defensive maneuvers were necessary—I envisioned crossbows and great vats of boiling oil that poured upon the attackers below. The view was splendid, encompassing the front of the castle and its moat, the tiled roofs of the town, the massive Gothic cathedral in the distance, and the aqueduct down in the valley below us. I was impressed by the bird's-eye perspective and squinted to see details in the distance.

Then, I noticed that Gramps looked piqued and maybe just a little faint. The ruddiness was gone from his cheeks, and his eyes were vacant. After the first glance, he took several steps back and would not approach the battlement.

"Umm, Gramps? Do you want to go back down?"

He nodded, apparently too frightened even to speak.

I felt helpless when I saw his reaction, never having been in such a position before. Looking around, I found we were nearly alone atop the tower, and no one else looked particularly disposed toward assisting us. We were far too high for me to communicate with my father on the ground far below. It was clear that getting my grandfather back down was going to be entirely up to me. I couldn't even run down the steps to get help. Gramps appeared far too distressed for me to leave him up there, even for a short time.

Taking his meaty hand, which was sweaty and cool, I led him to the stairs. The ancient stone steps were time-worn and hemmed in by sheer walls. I didn't know quite what to do but figured that if I could assist him in going down the series of steep staircases in a slow, controlled manner, he would be all right. At least he couldn't see very far down, as the individual flights were short, and as we descended, we would quickly approach a wall, then turn to proceed down the next flight.

I had visions of him toppling forward and both of us tumbling to the bottom. There was a black iron chain to grasp for stabilization. This passed through iron rings held fast to the walls, but there were no actual railings or banisters. While we were walking up, I had not foreseen what a problem this might be on the way down.

"Just hold my hand, Gramps. Grab my hand!"

But he didn't want to hold on to me. My poor grandfather put his back up against the wall and clutched the chain, grasping it as though he wanted to pull it out of the wall. He inched down the steps, taking deep breaths as I led the way. He wouldn't even consider releasing his grasp of the chain to clasp onto me. I coaxed him down, step by step, surprised by the fear in his usually confident features. I stood below him throughout the descent, pressing my meager weight against his bulging abdomen.

"I've got you. You won't fall. I won't let you fall."

My assurances did little to encourage him, but we made steady progress. I was grateful that no one was coming up the narrow stairway at the same time.

When we emerged from the stairwell, my mother, father, and grandmother were waiting expectantly. The impatience melted away, quickly replaced by concern as soon as they saw Gramps's face. Except for my grandmother, who looked on angrily, little sympathy to offer.

"Chuck, what the hell did you think you were doing? You know you're terrified of heights!"

He was cowed, and shook his head slowly. Then, he looked back up at the battlements that crowned the tower. "I didn't think it was that high." Gramps then smiled engagingly at me and declared, "Boy, I'm sure glad you was along for that one!"

A warmth welled within me; I was delighted by his compliment. I hadn't saved the paralyzed lizard that had recently appeared in my life, but I had helped my grandfather out of a truly precarious situation.

We took time for a picnic lunch on a grassy space in a nearby park, where my mother had spread a blanket and laid out the food.

"Great country, ain't it, Steverino?" Gramps asked me, repeating one of his favorite lines as he peeled the shell off a hard-boiled egg. He wasn't even in his own country, but he sure knew how to be appreciative. His thankfulness was an important life lesson for me, one that he drove home many times over the years.

Fourteen

Saying goodbye to my grandparents filled me with sadness as they prepared to return to Pittsburgh. Their visit served as a heartwarming reminder of the rest of my family back in the U.S. and how much we missed the relatives on both my father's side and my mother's. Cousins, aunts, uncles, and grandparents played a more important role in my life than I had realized until we left them behind.

But there were pressing matters to attend to right in Royal Oaks. We were now well into the school year, and Mr. Walden had become more demanding of us, as he had suggested he would be.

"Steven, I like your report," he said one day in early November as he walked around the class returning our papers, amply marked with corrections and suggestions from his red pen.

I could tell there was a "but" coming just from the tone of his voice.

He stood directly before me, looked at me affably, and gently pronounced his judgment. "But I just don't think *Danny Dunn and the Smallifying Machine* is challenging enough for the fifth grade. And I know you can read at a higher level. "

This startled me. My beloved teacher did not feel that the books I chose each week were sufficiently demanding. I had become fond of a series of books in which the main character was an intrepid redheaded boy just about my age, who was adventurous, intensely curious, and constantly getting into (and out of) trouble.

Hurt by his critique despite his kind delivery, I waited quietly for what he would say next.

"I have a list of books you could read, if you want to see them. Just come see me before lunch."

The situation was embarrassing, and I felt ashamed, especially as this conversation took place in front of everyone else in the classroom, though no one seemed to notice. As we were dismissed, I went up to his desk, and he handed me the list, his warm gray eyes meeting my own, a pleased expression on his face.

"Steven, take a look at this list of books. They are filled with adventure, and humor, and wonderful characters." He looked at me more seriously for a moment. "They can change your life."

I fidgeted a bit. That sounded like a tall order, but I wanted to show Mr. Walden that I was anxious to improve myself, and I reached for the paper. I was touched that he cared enough to single me out and encourage me to do better. He had that same attitude, it seemed, toward all of us: He provided a kindly invitation to stretch to a higher plane of comprehension and interpretation, and this I vowed I would do.

"Thanks, Mr. Walden."

He returned to his work, but I could tell he was satisfied with the encounter.

Over the ensuing weeks, I made it a point to obtain and read some of the books on his list. Plowing through several of the recommended stories, I found myself working harder to read the more complex books, thinking about them more, identifying more strongly with the characters and their situations, and taking lessons away from detailed conflict resolutions. One of the books, *A Wrinkle in Time*, was a classic science fiction story. It was longer and more intricate than most of the stories I was used to, with a more nuanced storyline. When I wrote my report, I repeatedly re-read parts of the book to ensure the accuracy of my answers to the requisite questions, something I hadn't needed to do before.

"What are you doing, Tom?" my father asked, approaching the kitchen table as I put the finishing touches on my report. "It's almost nine o'clock."

That was pretty late for me to be up on a school night.

"Just getting this report done. Mr. Walden asked me to read books that are more difficult."

He looked amused. "Tough teacher, huh?" I could tell he was pleased about this situation by the tone of his voice.

"Well, yeah. Tougher than my other teachers were, like Mrs. Smith and Mrs. Allen. But I *like* him. You know?"

He sat down across from me. "Oh, I know. I had a philosophy professor who pushed us very hard, just last year. I didn't like philosophy, and I didn't think I needed to understand it—it was just way out there."

Dad had been taking extension classes through the University of Maryland. This arrangement existed for servicemen right there on the air base. While unlikely to affect his rank in the Air Force, he felt it would improve his application when he retired in a few years and applied for a civilian job. I once attempted to read some of the entries in his philosophy textbook but found it completely incomprehensible. Even the introductory sentences were beyond my understanding.

He sat beside me and continued. "The more this professor made me do—readings, papers, quizzes, homework—the more I appreciated the subject. I began to really understand what he was trying to teach me. Because I was making such an effort, the lessons started to actually make sense. And then a light bulb went off—philosophy doesn't have to be some deep subject that only the most brilliant men can understand. It can actually show us how to think about life, even in the everyday world. It's not just for classrooms. I got a B in the class even though I figured, after the first time the class met, I would probably fail. That instructor brought me up a notch. He made me a better student."

I nodded my head vigorously. "Yeah. Mr. Walden is like that."

"Well, you're in the fifth grade now. Teachers are going to ask more of you, and it will get more challenging each year. They have to get you ready to think and reason and extract information on your own—you'll need to do that in college. The professors just put the lessons and work out there, and then they leave it up to you to do the learning. Mr. Walden is getting you started on the right foot."

Most nights, my father would lie beside me on my bed and read until I was nearly asleep. I didn't necessarily need bedtime stories to sleep; we simply fancied spending father-son time this way. After a visit to the big library on base, I'd have books on anatomy and physiology, horses, dogs, jet planes, and the adventures of dauntless little boys. I had a lot of questions about the books we read, but my father was patient and thoughtful as he answered me.

Whether genuine or not, Dad showed enthusiasm for the books we shared, his voice somehow carrying me into the story as it took hold in my imagination. As we read *The Black Stallion*, I was Alex, unafraid of the powerful horse, clinging tightly to his mane as we escaped from some dangerous pursuer or took the lead in a race in which the stakes were impossibly high. I bit my lip with profound sorrow and blinked back tears when the sheriff's men shot Sounder, and I searched, in my imagination, as eagerly and hopefully to find that wounded dog as his owner did. When Black Beauty collapsed from exhaustion, I was there, kneeling beside him, urging him to get up and desperately trying to provide solace to the prostrate beast.

I lived a life of adventure and fulfillment during those quiet hours in my bedroom.

"Can you see it?" I asked my father one evening as we reclined on the bed in the dim light of my bedroom.

"See what?"

"You know, Dad. Your blind spot."

"How could I see a blind spot? It's . . . blind."

I pulled my head up off the pillow. "But the book talks about some sort of spot, something you can see, like a hole, in the middle of your vision. Here, let me try."

I held the book at the described distance from my eyes, then moved it back and forth several times. "There!"

My father, just beginning to doze off, startled awake. He turned towards me and frowned.

"Dad, this is so cool. It's a missing part of my vision from the part of my retina where the optic nerve comes in. See, see? Look over here at this diagram."

I was elated, repeatedly trying to recreate the odd phenomenon in my visual field. He rubbed his eyes and tried to look impressed.

"This book is full of amazing facts, Tom."

It sounded like a statement that would precede his closing the book and heading off to bed.

"I know, Dad! Remember the chapter on the ear? And those little hair cells that turn sound vibrations into electricity so the brain can hear?"

"Yup. Who knew they could get so much interesting information into *Eyes, Ears, Nose and Throat: How We Function*? But now I'm afraid I have to get off to my bedroom and get some sleep. My own eyes and ears are ready to shut down."

With that, he yawned, turned off the light, and bade me a good night.

An almost magical collection of auspicious factors came to bear upon me in that year: the books I enjoyed with my father at home, my own development as a reader at the behest of Mr. Walden, the variety of topics and subjects I was exposed to in school, and the rich historic environment of Spain. All of this cultivated within me a new sense of curiosity and a strong desire to learn. Even as I continued to struggle in social and athletic pursuits, there was an element of personal growth. I began to dream of professional success and of contributing to society. This new-found interest in academic success surprised my father, and perhaps my mother as well. Much later in my life, I came to understand how much I benefited from the conjunction at this time of all of these factors that aided me in my intellectual maturation.

I pulled out the flashlight I kept hidden under my bed so I could read some more after Dad went to sleep. Flipping open my favorite volume of the encyclopedia, I found the section on the human body.

"Humerus," I whispered, making sure I pronounced it correctly. "Radius, ulna. Carpal bones. Metacarpals . . . phalanges."

Again and again, I arranged the anatomy transparencies, one atop the next, trying to understand how all the parts fit together, set on committing to memory the names and shapes of the bones, muscles, and organs.

Fifteen

The observance of the Christmas holiday was more subdued among the Spanish than the highly commercial affair we were used to in the States. Still, those of us stationed in Spain celebrated as eagerly as our families and fellow citizens across the Atlantic.

Like any ten-year-old, I counted the days as they passed in early November, waiting eagerly for the bliss of the holiday season. At school, the classrooms filled with decorations. Holiday art projects adorned the windows, from construction paper cornucopias to impish pilgrims gathered at the table for their feasts, to cotton ball snowmen and drawings of verdant Christmas trees sagging with ornaments, ribbons, and stars. I was mindful, in looking over these artistic expressions, of the festive homes featured in the Sears and JC Penney catalogs I had been drooling over for the past few months.

"How many more days?" I asked each night at dinner. I didn't have to qualify what I was asking about.

"One less than yesterday," my mother answered, urging me to eat.

In school, we focused on the Spanish Christmas customs. Learning their celebratory songs was one of the most enjoyable aspects of Spanish culture. Translations of hymns such as "Silent Night" enabled our understanding of the language. Even complex words seemed to resonate in my mind, as they were set to tunes I knew well. We joyously sang favorite

Spanish carols, like "Alegría" and "Capitán de Madera," even though we may have been a little sketchy on the meaning of the words.

One afternoon, after I came home from school, Mrs. Reimolds called my mother, inviting me for dinner and to make Christmas ornaments with TC. There was just a bit of a chill in the air, enough to make us fantasize about the white Christmas we might have seen in our hometowns back in the States.

TC and I confided in each other, outlining our respective wish lists for the holiday. I was surprised that, even at her young age, she was beginning to turn her attention to clothes and accessories, with less emphasis on toys. I considered such things nuisances, especially when they were presented as gifts, since they were displacing something of much higher value in my world that would provide entertainment or fun. But I had begun to appreciate, as I observed TC and our older sisters, that the mystery, the gaiety, the unmatched felicity of Christmas could not stand against the staid and boring realities of life forever. I knew that, sooner or later, I'd be asking for a new pair of pants or a sweater vest. But for now, the Yuletide remained the highlight of the entire year, eclipsing virtually every other source of happiness.

Like ours, the Reimolds home was aglow with miniature lights and had festive, decorative scenes on several of the tabletops. TC's mother had a talent for making ceramics, which she created in a workshop on the Air Force base. Mrs. Reimolds presented Christmas decorations to our family that we cherished for a generation. One of these was a ceramic evergreen tree with little holes on the outer edges of the boughs. In each of these holes, we placed a small plastic, conical bead shape that resembled a light. There was a light bulb in the hollow base of the tree, and when it was turned on, the little tree appeared to have strings of colored lights upon it. I would sometimes just sit and stare at it, lost in the magic of the holiday.

"So Steven," Mrs. Reimolds began, holding up a white foam sphere and some plastic needle caps that had been scavenged from the hospital. "Here's how you make the ornament: you take these caps and push them into the foam, like this."

She demonstrated what TC and I were supposed to do. Once we had constructed the ornament, we smeared it with white glue and sprinkled it with glitter. I colored the first in scintillating red and held it up for inspection. It had the appearance, I'm sure, of a shiny Styrofoam ball covered with glittering red needle caps, but in my eyes, it was as alluring as the Bethlehem star.

"That'll look beautiful on your tree." TC was beaming.

I couldn't help but share her enthusiasm. I didn't get to come to her house very often, at least not by myself. When our families gathered at the table or in conversational groups, I didn't get much one-on-one time with TC or her mom. But that night, the two of them devoted their time and attention to me in a way that made me feel especially important.

TC also made some ornaments, which sparkled in green, silver, and red, and we hurried into the living room to put them on their tree. They looked conspicuously homemade, but we loved them all the more for it, and they reflected the lights wound around the tree, accenting the illumination that made the scene so magical in our eyes.

You don't ever forget making Christmas ornaments with someone. I don't remember what her mom made for dinner that evening or what her dad said when he came home, grinning at the products of our efforts. But I know that I went home with a greater sense of delight in the Christmas season. And perhaps a greater appreciation for my own creativity, buoyed as I was by their affection.

There was a shared culture in the United States in those years, imbued through the entire nation by radio and newspapers, periodicals, and television broadcasting, long before the fragmentation that arrived with cable TV, social media, and the internet. But overseas families were isolated from this American experience. The sense of a national community did not extend to troops and their families on U.S. military bases scattered around the world. We felt separated from the American cultural milieu, and we missed it. No period of the year affected our sympathies as much as the holiday season. Still, as with all shared deprivation, the mutual suffering forged a stronger bond between those who bore it.

None of the local television stations were broadcasting in English, and watching Spanish stations was unfulfilling for those of us who understood and spoke at only a very elementary level. But when we had the opportunity, we listened loyally to the American songs, trends, and preferences that made their way into our insular world. The Department of Defense offered Armed Forces Radio—a tightly controlled broadcasting medium that bordered on propaganda—to keep us entertained. AFR offered Top Forty tunes, home-grown entertainment, and news stories, including human interest anecdotes and results of sporting contests, both on the air base and in the larger military community in Europe. The station played the most popular songs of the day, so music was one experience that closely aligned us with contemporary American culture.

During Christmas, one of the local DJs would showcase his well-honed impression of the character "Alvin" from the popular Chipmunks characters as he painstakingly read the Christmas wishes of scores of kids whose parents helped them draft letters to Santa's workshop. Each evening for several weeks after Thanksgiving, we'd snap on the radio while cleaning up the kitchen, doing homework, or taking care of other chores and listen to the letters he'd selected. The silly voice he utilized and the heartfelt sentiments he expressed drew us closer together and lent a sense of community to our holiday in that corner of the world.

We sat, filled with anticipation, waiting to hear who wanted what. There was enough gossip, and the community was small enough, that you could recognize at least some of the people "Alvin" was talking about, even though he only used first names.

". . . and Andrea, who is nine years old, wants a new Barbie doll, a Monopoly game, and an Easy-Bake Oven. And she wants to wish a Merry Christmas to her grandma and grandpa and cousins back in Frankfurt, Kentucky."

The DJ would pause between each letter as if to give us all a chance to figure out whose list he was sharing. He had a funny way of referring to our housing plan as "Royal-eee Oaks," in the spirit of Alvin, which amused us even more. Kathy and I grew wistful as we thought about our friends and neighbors, who, like us, were wishing they could be back in their hometowns, or at least somewhere in the States, for the holidays.

"My friend Christine has a little sister named Andrea," my sister said to the rest of us as we listened for the next person on the list. "They're from Kentucky—I'll bet it's them. I'll ask her at school."

"I have a letter," he continued, through a backdrop of soft static, "from Peter, also in Royal-eee Oaks, who wants a baseball bat and glove, a slot car racing set, and for his dad to get home from TDY by Christmas Eve."

The Air Force frequently sent its members on temporary duty—TDY, they called it—to wherever they were needed, whenever they deemed it necessary, even over the holidays. Duty was duty for the Department of Defense, regardless of the season. The prior year, my father had returned from a weeklong trip to Germany on Christmas Eve, just in the nick of time, to celebrate the holiday with us.

I often yearned for the DJ to read my wishes on that radio show. I imagined him reading my list and that my friends, who were bound to be listening, would laugh with their families because they knew who Steven was since he wanted those trains. Curiously, though, I never sent a letter. I guess I was too shy to risk occupying that stage, even though it was merely a local radio show.

In our house, the Christmas decorations, which we pulled out with great urgency despite my mother's call for patience, had not changed much in all the years I could remember. However, they still evoked enthusiasm and excitement for the Yuletide season. We had an artificial tree made of aluminum, with thin, silver, tinsel-like fronds projecting from wire "branches" of different lengths, each of which fit into a particular slot within a large pasteboard box. My mother had worked at Sears and Roebuck when we lived in Cumberland, just before Dad went to Vietnam. All of our decorations, and probably the vast majority of our housewares, came from that store. My role during the tree-assembly process was to pull the different-length branches out of the box and hand them to my mother and sister, who pushed them into the appropriate, color-coded holes in the round wooden trunk while my father assessed the assembly to make certain the tapered shape of the tree was evolving perfectly.

Somehow, my sister and I always seemed to get into arguments about the process.

"Hand me *that* one, Steve!"

"No, you're not ready for that one," I'd snap. "*This* is the one for that row."

My sister was quite a bit bigger than I, and though she was thin, she usually got the better of me in both arguments and our few physical encounters. I often ended up sullen and obedient after a spat. But I knew I was growing up and would hold my own someday.

My mother would adjudicate our disputes, her large dark eyes sparkling with impatience and frustration. Sometimes, she would simply threaten us when her patience had reached its limits. After years of working in retail sales, she was far less joyful about the holidays than we were. Even my father was more jubilant during the decorating than she was.

"I'll get the belt!" she would eventually yell, and that was the end of our fighting.

My mother wasn't especially cross, but when disobedience and lack of interpersonal respect went unchecked by her pointed suggestions, she could become downright intimidating. And she would carry out her threats, as we had unfortunately learned many times when we tested her limits. Some colorful swearing usually preceded any physical sanctions, so we had a clear borderline from which to retreat, a marker Kathy and I had learned to recognize and respect.

Once we assembled the tree, with a few replacements and swaps among the branches, we began decorating. This family activity lacked the color and jubilance that the typical Currier and Ives scene might suggest since all of our ornaments consisted of identical round blue bulbs, with a lone blue star to place atop the silver sprig that projected straight up from the top of the wooden trunk, like a radio antenna.

I might have been disappointed if that had been the entire complement of our Christmas tree decor. But there was a special accessory that made our tree a true joy to behold.

My sister eyed me curiously as she cleaned up after our decorating. "What are you doing?"

I sat gleefully on couch, facing the Christmas tree. "Look at those colors. Don't you love those colors?"

I was transfixed by the spectacle in front of me. Every few seconds, our silver tree took on a new hue. Dad had placed a spotlight at the base of the tree, and to its front was affixed to a multicolored disk that slowly revolved in front of the lamp, casting colorful shafts of light onto the tree, one after the next, for hours on end.

To sit in the darkened living room and observe this ever-changing, color-enhanced spectacle was a wondrous experience for me.

Kathy was not so impressed. "Well, turn it off and go to bed. It's late."

I yawned and stretched, turning off the color wheel. But the Christmas season was becoming more magical with each passing day.

Sixteen

As winter approached, temperatures dropped in the arid lands outside of Madrid, one of Europe's highest capitals. The lizards were sluggish and far less numerous. We'd still see them sunning on the walls, but they weren't lying out much down in the gullies. During the cool season, while kicking along the paths or playing army in the trenches, it was unusual for us to scare up one of the brownies or rat-tails. We assumed they stayed in their holes and shivered, coming out occasionally to grab whatever snack was available.

Just before Christmas, Mark, Mike, and I met for a half-hearted attempt to track some of them down. The conversation centered on Christmas as we visited our favored ambush sites. It had been many weeks since we'd caught a lizard, and the fulfillment of keeping a few of them, however briefly, was something we missed.

"What do you think you're getting?" I asked Mark.

"Well, probably a sweater and some new pants. My pants all have holes in the knees."

"I mean fun stuff. What Santa brings—you know, toys and games and things!"

Mike echoed my sentiments. "Yeah, Mark. It's Christmas. There's gotta be something better than pants and sweaters!"

"I asked for a Monopoly game," he acknowledged. "And this great Matchbox ambulance with a little bed that comes out. And it has a battery so the red light comes on! And a model of an aircraft carrier. Plus a football."

"How about you?" I asked Mike.

We'd reviewed our selections a few times before, but they were constantly changing, especially as we thumbed through the catalogs. Discussing them over and over made things more exciting, as though describing them aloud would improve our chances of receiving them.

Mike stuck his foot into a sage bush and rattled it around in the dead leaves at the base. Nothing happened.

"I need a new bike most of all," he said. A bike was a tall order for most of us, so we were a bit awed at how matter-of-factly he stated this. "And I asked for a *Jungle Book* record."

Mike and I had spent many happy hours listening to his album of Disney's *Lady and the Tramp*.

"Plus, I'm hoping for some airplane models, some books, and a basketball with a hoop."

It was my turn. They both looked at me expectantly.

"I like trains," I began.

"We know that!" Mark laughed.

He'd played with my HO train set at my house many times, and I was simply enchanted when his father set up his trains on the living room floor, with diesel engines and steamers, freight trains and magical silver passenger consists, crisscrossing each other on trestles and bridges. Mr. Godwin collected German Märklin trains: expensive, fine-tuned, and reliable, they were a far cry from the mass-market Japanese models I played with.

"So what'd you ask for?" Mike asked impatiently.

"There's this little station house in Toyland at the BX. It's from Germany, and it has a waiting platform with little people and suitcases, and a ticket window, and a big clock, and it lights up!"

"Neat," Mark mused.

"I saw it—it's pretty cool," Mike added.

"And there's this crossing signal that lights up with red lights when the train goes by, just like the real ones. I can put cars right on the tracks until the train comes, and when the lights come on . . . pull them off just in the nick of time!"

I'd seen something like that in a movie when a group of nuns stalled a school bus in the path of an oncoming train, and I was dying to replicate it.

"That's it?" Mike said, a little disappointed.

"No, lots more! There's this castle with knights on horses and catapults in the Sears catalog, and a big World War II attack set with Germans and Americans and tanks and machine guns. I saw a model of a B-17 Flying Fortress that comes with German Fighters and a base that looks like a miniature city, with factories and a river—you put the bomber way up high over the base, and the fighters come in from behind, like a bombing run. And I asked for a model of the USS *Enterprise*. It has a bunch of little fighter planes on the flight deck, ready to launch. Oh, yeah, and I want to get a football set, with a jersey and helmet and pads."

I had overwhelmed them.

"Anything else?" Mark asked a little sarcastically. I think he regarded me as kind of spoiled, since his family had so many more children. I'm sure he expected that to be the end of my list.

"Well," I added, "the last time we were playing army, I broke the muzzle on my Johnny Eagle M-16. So I'm hoping to get a new one."

Changing the subject back to the matter before us, Mike gestured toward the gullies. "It'd be nice to catch a few lizards before it gets too cold."

He hadn't spent much time hunting with us, but he was now interested. I was glad to consider him a colleague in our effort to catch as many of the little reptiles as possible, even if we just let them go the next day. And, most importantly, I was pleased that he'd been enlisted in the mission to find and capture the fabled six-lined racerunner, the lizard we could never seem to find. By reputation, this little guy was far too fast and clever to be corralled by just two boys. We'd need at least three.

"I don't think we'll see many lizards till it gets warm next spring," I said, disappointed. "But we'll really rev it up then. We'll comb these gullies until we find one of the six-lines. I know they're out there!"

I thought longingly of the day when I had encountered one, or at least believed that I had—the creature tore through the underbrush and right past my foot, staggering me with its speed. But I was convinced I'd seen its fine yellow pinstripes ablaze on its black body as it left me flat-footed and slack-jawed, agog at its capabilities.

"Oh sure, we'll find one," Mark replied with more than a twinge of sarcasm. "Haven't you been saying that for the last two years?"

He looked doubtfully at Mike, who shrugged. He was not well-acquainted with the shortcomings of our crusade.

"Yeah, I know."

This reflection on our failures put me on the spot, as I was the self-proclaimed leader of this little band. We'd had little success in our most important mission, and this was surely a reflection of my ability to inspire the team.

"Look, we still have six months to find one."

Neither of them looked very optimistic as I tried to encourage them.

Disappointed by our failures, my friends and I shuffled back to our adjoining driveways. Worried, I didn't speak for a bit. Whenever I took charge of things, it seemed like disappointment was the order of the day. My few forays into leadership had not ended well, at least those I could remember. When obstacles presented themselves, I struggled. As negative feedback emerged, I lost faith in myself. It became a self-fulfilling cycle.

But I couldn't let that happen with our quest for the six-lined racerunner. I had to deliver. Somehow.

We said our goodnights and headed for our homes.

The twilight was beginning to envelop us, and as I walked up the short hill to our unit, someone inside turned on the porch lights. We had a pair of red-and-white striped plastic candles that stood on either side of the front door, nearly as tall as me. When plugged in, these glowed a warm, rosy color. No one else in our neighborhood had anything quite like them. I was captivated by these oversize symbols of the season, and they, together with the silver Christmas tree in the front window, curiously alight in red, then green, then blue, then yellow, somehow embodied all that was good about Christmas in our modest home.

I walked in to find my mom serving dinner.

"Sit down, bud," she said, placing several plates on the table.

"Tacos?" I asked, immediately excited.

Our version of tacos was unlike the standard Tex-Mex version. Mom had worked diligently with a friend when we were stationed in Japan to perfect a Cuban recipe. She made her own tortillas from cornstarch, while Kathy and I often helped cut the dough into little circles. After cooking ground beef and onions, my mother placed a mixture of the two inside each circle of dough, folding them over and crimping the edges. She fried them in oil until golden, then popped them onto the table. While they were piping hot, we'd cut them open and stuff them with cheese, lettuce, tomato and Tabasco sauce. The evening instantly became festive when these were on the menu.

"So, tell me about school today." My father handed me a taco without onions—I was the picky one, which probably explained my slight build.

"Señorita Ares came and talked to us about Christmas in Spain."

"Did you learn anything new?"

Things had become quiet while we all stuffed the tacos, trying to keep the steam from burning our fingertips.

I sighed with the first bite. Maybe our "tacos" were just a Cuban version of the cheeseburger, but I loved them.

"I guess so. You know, they don't make such a big deal out of Christmas, with lights and presents and all. She said that for them, Christmas is a much more religious holiday, without all the shopping. But they like to place a manger scene somewhere in the house where everyone can see, like the one Mrs. Reimolds made for us. And they have dinners with the family, and parties, too, like we do. But I guess they keep it a little quieter to make sure the birth of Jesus is the most important part. And church. Church is a big part of it."

"Makes sense," my mother agreed.

"I'd miss all those presents!" I couldn't fathom Christmas morning without presents under the tree.

"Well, yeah, but they get to all that later, right?" My sister chimed in.

"First it's New Year's. Spanish people love to go out on New Year's— like when you go to the Plaza Mayor and eat those grapes, huh, Dad?"

The Spaniards in Madrid converged on the sprawling plaza in the old quarter late on New Year's Eve, and when the great clock struck twelve, each consumed a single grape at every chime. Or at least tried.

"I almost got all twelve in last year." Dad nodded in agreement. He loved those kinds of traditions. Luckily, he had my mom along to keep him from partying too much.

"It's supposed to be good luck," she reminded us.

"I think if you're really full of wine and tapas, it can't be too easy to eat twelve grapes so fast." Kathy pushed her plate away, opting out of the last taco. Eating three of them usually meant lying down after supper to digest. "Are you going this year with the Mazzas? Can Marie and I come?"

"Hah!" My father patted her heartily on the top of her head. "Maybe in seven years. Right now, you, Marie, and Robbie should go to the teen club and drink Seven-Up while they spin records."

She looked disheartened. Kathy fancied herself more grown-up than she actually was.

"So then," I continued, "about a week later, on Three Kings Day, they celebrate with presents, especially for the kids. The night before, they put their shoes by the front door, and in the night, the Three Kings come and cover them with presents."

"Why shoes?"

I was puzzled about that. "I can't remember."

"What about Santa?" Kathy asked. She knew I was hovering on the brink of losing my belief in the magic of Santa Claus.

"Spanish kids don't believe in Santa Claus. And if you don't believe, well, I guess he doesn't come." That was the best I could come up with.

"Maybe the spirit of Santa shows up in the form of the Three Kings." Mom tried to reconcile things for my benefit

"Here's the best part: they're off from school the whole time—all the way until Three Kings Day!"

I couldn't help but think of how much fun my friends and I could have with our new stuff in that extra week off. The Spaniards had definitely planned it right.

Seventeen

"Ready, Steve-O?" My mother stood in the hallway, impatiently waiting for me.

We were preparing to go into Madrid on a Friday night to enjoy some tapas in our favorite neighborhood bar.

"They don't really do lights for Christmas, do they?" My mother made this statement every year that we lived in Spain. Things hadn't changed.

"Christmas is different here, Mom."

But there was no shortage of merriment, which was the case on most weekend nights in Madrid, and probably most of the weekdays, as well. We sat in the warm, dimly lit tavern, enjoying the scents of Spanish cuisine and the earthy atmosphere.

"Can we go to Woolworths?"

Dad nodded, not surprised by my request. It was enjoyable to browse the aisles and see what might enhance our Christmas spirit.

While I always enjoyed perusing the toy aisles in that store, the Christmas season offered something even better: the creches. Miniature nativity scenes dominated an entire department of the store. There were dozens, maybe hundreds of them, of all shapes, sizes, and levels of intricacy. Some were tiny, with only a few figures huddled inside a miniature stable; others were so vast and expansive, with many figurines and animals, that they could have covered an entire living room floor. These magnificent sets adorned the homes of well-to-do Spanish men, perhaps bankers or businessmen. As I made my way down the aisle, peering at each scene in turn, my parents tried to hustle me along.

"Well, that's enough for this year," my father said, his patience wearing thin. He wasn't quite as enthusiastic about miniatures as I was.

"You know, Steve, we have our own nativity scene at home," my mother reminded me.

Mrs. Reimolds, in one of her many acts of kindness and generosity, had fired us an extensive group of figurines to gather beneath our tree, centered upon a small homemade wooden stable my dad had assembled. I took great pains to arrange them just so each year: the Holy Family, shepherds, wise men, angels, and a fitting group of animals. The entire set was of the glossiest white, and each figure reflected those beautiful colors from the spinning spotlight, a coveted part of my Christmas experience.

"Course, Mom. I just thought we could get something to make it a little more realistic."

I found my mark: a few spindly, leafless model trees. These, I thought, would be perfect around the manger scene my father had created for the figurines.

"See? Won't these look great?"

They both nodded, hoping to head to the checkout stand.

We weren't the only ones out in search of more Christmas spirit. The festive aisles were alive with admiring Spaniards, as eager as I to see what the store laid out. I watched families having animated discussions about what new piece or figure to add to the scene that graced their homes, creating sets that would continue to grow, year in and year out.

"See, Mom? Everybody wants a more realistic scene under the tree."

She sighed and smiled half-heartedly, looking at my father.

As I watched these Spanish families, I realized that the items they were looking at were not just toys or knick-knacks to them. The creche in each home was a simple statement about the importance of religion as the center of the Christmas holiday. Spain's population was still in large part Catholic, although church attendance was continually falling. The failure to attend Mass did not affect the close alignment of culture with the Catholic religion.

As much as I loved Christmas and all that came with it, I eventually understood that the *anticipation* of the pleasure I would experience was often more enjoyable than the event itself since, paradoxically, one can never fulfill the expectation of perfection. It is a clever person, I now realize, who learns to tease himself with expectation while at the same time tempering anticipation with realism. At that age, I was merely beginning to discover that the enjoyment of life was an exercise in attitude management, and the energies I expended in Christmas-wishing made this plain. Admittedly, I was then still cradled within a mantle of enthusiasm for the holiday that knew no bounds. I could not yet speak plainly to myself about the inevitable shortcomings of an event that I expected to provide almost unattainable heights of happiness and fulfillment.

But even in my naivete, I had started to experience the greatest amount of joy on the threshold of the holiday. This was on the sacred night of Christmas Eve, in which people gathered to feast, to share food and libations and goodwill, then come together in a church or chapel to sing, pray, and rejoice. Perhaps it wasn't the anticipation of happiness that kept me awake until the wee hours, but rather the realization that I simply could not feel any more euphoric on Christmas day, as the hours slipped slowly away, than I did on that festive night. This was a wisdom that evolved and crystallized in my later adolescence, when the social aspects of the holiday finally began to outweigh the importance of the gifts I received.

"It's here! It's finally here!" I was literally skipping through the kitchen, bubbling with enthusiasm about our Christmas Eve celebration.

By the time the day arrived, I'm sure I'd nearly driven my parents crazy. I was so anxious with anticipation, so consumed with joyful speculation, that every moment seemed suspended in time, each day passing with excruciating slowness.

But finally, it was time for unrestrained elation. We'd eaten dinner, and Mom had lifted the moratorium on candy canes and Christmas cookies. I indulged in a fair share of these treats, their sugary essence suffusing through me, further piquing my boundless joy.

"I said *one*," my mother cautioned as I helped myself to the sugar cookies.

I'd already had three, but the warning served to slow me down. While my mother prepared food for the open house, I gazed longingly at the presents under the tree. Anticipating some important additions to my railroad setup, I laid out the tracks for my model train set on the floor in my room, and placed the dark green locomotive on the tracks at the head of a colorful group of freight cars. I scattered the houses and stores around one end to create the nidus of a town, which I imagined would be dependent on the railroad for its economic vitality.

While I watched the short train chase itself around the loop, the circle of track became, in my mind, a branch off the mainline of the Pennsylvania Railroad, which hosted mile-long freights through the midsection of its home state, on multiple busy tracks, with diesel engines and steam-powered locomotives putting their enormous power to work over the mountains of the Keystone State. The Pennsylvania Railroad was my favorite line, primarily because of the many trains it carried daily through Pittsburgh.

Mark stopped in to see me that afternoon, and I led him into my room.

"See, the town is right on the outskirts of Pittsburgh. It's part of the Pennsylvania Railroad. Pretend the tracks go into the city, right along the big river, to the steel mills and cement factories."

I carefully arranged my Matchbox cars and the few tiny figurines I had, hoping the community would expand the next day when I received my gifts, and that the town's citizens would be rendered safe from the speeding trains by the addition of a railroad crossing signal.

"It just looks like a little town." Mark wasn't afraid to burst my bubble.

"Well, wait till tomorrow! There'll be more buildings and places for the train to stop."

I didn't understand why he couldn't appreciate my vision. But he promised to come back for the party in the evening.

Guests began to arrive at our home, and the joy that emanates from groups of tipsy adults spread. Throughout the course of the evening, groups of friends and neighbors stopped by. The Reimoldses came early and partied with us all evening. The Mazzas popped up from downstairs, and I proudly showed Mike my new village. Mark returned as promised, and the three of us labored long over the arrangement of the buildings and accessories in my little town.

In no time, I had to bid a fond Merry Christmas to Mark and Mike, who were off to other gatherings. Afterward, TC and I drank kiddie cocktails, which we were free to concoct with Seven-Up and maraschino cherries at the kitchen counter, and munched on Christmas cookies. My mother's frosted sugar cookies came in all sorts of fun, festive shapes. Kathy and I lovingly decorated these with glitter, colorful sprinkles, or silver balls that dissolved into little sugar spheres if you sucked on them. The cookies were always moist and fresh just before the holiday, and the icing slightly crunchy on the outside. This frosting, along with the crunchy sprinkles or glitter, contrasted perfectly with the soft texture of the cookies. Given a dozen of them, I could make them disappear in a few minutes.

"Did you help your mom with these?" TC asked, looking at the room full of chattering people.

"Well, yeah." I held one up, admiring it. "I helped decorate them. That's the fun part!"

I had trouble enough not to eat every cookie I decorated, but my sister would watch me closely while we made the cookies, reporting my activities carefully to my mother.

TC and I were kindred spirits, but not just because we shared Mr. Walden's classroom. We'd both been young and anxious when our fathers were deployed to Vietnam, a distant land of death and pestilence for

American service members. We each had borne silent witness to the gut-wrenching fear our mothers endured as the Tet Offensive swept through South Vietnam, chronicled nightly on the news, just as the two men arrived in theater.

"Were you lonely?" she asked me quietly as she peeled the sticky paper off a candy cane.

"Well, sort of. I mean, I had my mom and sister, plus Gram and Gramps. And my cousin Rick—he's my good friend. But I spent a lot of time just thinking about my dad. I had to walk to school by myself, since Rick was just in kindergarten. It always seemed like it was gray and cold, and I had to walk past two really big graveyards. I kept thinking about who was buried in there—so many tombstones!"

Conjuring that foreboding image in my mind, I continued.

"In Cumberland, my dad used to play baseball with me in the backyard. We had a plastic ball, and if I hit it just right, it would go all the way over the house. He got so excited! I loved those games. There was no one to make me feel that way when he was gone. I really missed him."

I knew TC's family moved to her aunt's house in Columbus when her dad shipped out. I looked over at her, waiting to hear her side of it.

"It was really different there. My mom seemed so sad all the time. I wanted to make her feel better, but I didn't know how. No one else in my school had a dad in Vietnam. They just didn't really care about it."

I nodded silently, thinking about what it was like to live in my grandmother's house. "On the dresser in the bedroom I shared with Ricky, Grandma had a picture of my mom and dad from right after they got married. I sat and looked at that picture every night before I went to sleep. I never knew how long a year could be—it seemed to go on forever. Over and over, I thought about how it was when we were all together, the four of us, in our house in Cumberland."

I couldn't express it to TC, but I thought that maybe it wasn't just loneliness that affected me during the year Dad was away—something else happened. I became more withdrawn, more introverted, more socially backward as those months dragged on. I fell a few steps behind the other boys when my father left. And maybe that's why I didn't quite measure up in boldness or aggressiveness or toughness, the traits other boys seemed to come by so naturally.

It was perhaps an unusual moment to compare notes on our shared experience. Before us, the room was filled with happy people eating, drinking, and talking as the festive music played and the crazy color wheel spun. Conviviality was the order of the evening, and it was infectious. In no time, TC and I were laughing together and talking about school.

As with all good things, the party seemed to wind down too quickly. We waved goodbye to the last of our friends, and I ran out to the terraza to watch TC pull away as her father's big car eased out of the driveway and turned for home.

"G'night! Merry Christmas!"

"C'mon, Kath—let's go!"

Midnight Mass was a revered tradition in our house for as long as I could remember. I wasn't allowed to stay up that late on any other night of the year, which made for unbridled excitement in the house. I grabbed a jacket and joined my family as we hustled down the stairs and into the Peugeot. Kathy was in the choir, so she had to arrive early.

"I wish we had stained-glass windows. I miss stained-glass windows," my sister lamented as we parked.

She and I had attended Catholic school before coming overseas. We went to Mass regularly during those years, not only on Sundays but also several times during the school week. The pageantry and the visual appeal of the services had become an essential aspect of the religious experience.

But our local church in Royal Oaks was a rather plain structure, which served as the school auditorium, movie theater, and nondenominational chapel. It was nothing like the one on the base, which had colorful windows with scenes from the Bible and an actual steeple. But we were content to attend "folk mass" in the nondescript hall by the elementary school in Royal Oaks.

The strains of a Christmas hymn played on a tinkling piano were barely audible as we got out of the car. Kathy rushed off to sing with her friends while we found seats. I was sleepy but enthused, and we sang every Christmas song I knew that evening, between the short preamble to the service, the Mass itself, and a short, animated sing-along afterward. I waved to a few friends, most of whom seemed as tired as I was. With my sister up on stage in front of us, singing her heart out, I appreciated the experience even more than I would have otherwise.

Kathy soon rejoined us. She looked like a Christmas angel to me with her blue satin robe, pretty smile, and long blond hair.

"Mom, can we have eggnog?" my sister asked.

"Well, OK. But only one eggnog, one present, and bed. Got it?" I'd forgotten that Mom allowed us to open one present on Christmas Eve.

Even when she was exhausted, my mother could be kindly and indulgent to her children.

We cheered and rushed out of the car moments later, bounding up the stairs to see who would be first. Kathy was taller and a bit faster, but I closed on her quickly as we reached the front door, and we burst through it in what was essentially a dead heat.

Hauling into the living room, I grabbed a box I'd staked out, shook it, read the tag, and let the paper fly. Mom always used pre-made bows, so they were easy to pull off and set aside to be used again the following year. I heard Kathy exclaim something about an outfit she'd been wanting, and I turned to see her holding it up against her tall, thin body.

"Perfect!" My mother beamed—apparently, it was the right size, color, and everything.

I turned back to my own package and, pulling the last shred of paper off, was greeted with an exquisite sight: a picture of a freight train moving past a railroad station, in front of which there flashed a pair of red warning lights, while a man in a pickup truck looked on, bemused, at the passing boxcars.

"It's the crossing signal!"

I was exultant. Pulling it from the box, I dashed into my room and connected it to the circle of track. Then, I eased the train around the loop of track. To my absolute delight, the red lights under the crossbuck sign flashed brightly as each train car rolled by. I darkened the room and threw myself on the floor to observe more closely. Pulling some cars and trucks from my carrying case, I lined them up by the track so they could wait impatiently in line for the train to go by. This was a delightful fulfill-ment of my boyish aspirations. For the ultimate demonstration, I placed a school bus directly on the track, waiting coyly for the train to approach.

"Watch this! Watch this!" I called to no one in particular.

Just as the red warning lights began to flash, I enacted the moment from the movie we'd seen, when the motor miraculously started. The bus jolted forward, carrying its passengers to safety. I'd waited months to recreate that scenario.

Mom appeared at the door. "Here's your eggnog, bud."

Dad followed and watched, amused at the spectacle that unfolded each time the train came around. "Wow," he said with practiced enthusi-asm. "Just like the real thing."

"Yeah! Just like the real thing!" I countered, barely able to contain myself.

In a few minutes, I was in bed, drowsing toward sleep. The locomo-tive had come to a stop just outside the town. But in my mind, over and over, the train approached the crossing, the diesel blew its air horn, the signal flashed a warning, and the traffic came to an obedient halt. My little town had come to life.

Eighteen

Mike, Mark, and I were sprawled on the living room floor at the Mazzas', playing board games as the holidays wound down. I had my chin in my hands, looking at Mike's big, green, artificial Christmas tree. I was captivated by the glowing lights nested among the branches. It was much prettier than our silver tree, especially in daylight.

"Sometimes I get sad after Christmas," I admitted to my friends.

"Yeah, me too," Mark agreed, and Mike nodded.

I felt sort of hollow each year in the days right after Christmas as I thought about returning to school, even though I'd been ecstatic with the gifts I received and the goodwill that prevailed at our feasts and parties.

"How many times can you run your train around the track and through that town? There's only so many ways to move the buildings around."

Mike was right. An uneasy sort of boredom had set in, no matter how much enjoyment I received from each of these individual actions. I had also played with all my other new gifts until the same sense of overuse came over me. Finally, exhausted with all of this self-indulgence, I had set off to play with my friends and see what new toys and distractions they had received.

"Did your dad put up his trains?" I asked Mark.

He rolled the dice, moved his turn, and shifted around a bit. "Well, yeah. But one of the steam engines is missing. He's on the warpath about it."

I shuddered; Mark's dad could get pretty riled up, and I determined not to head down there till he was in a good mood again. It was kind of funny to see a grown man running trains all over the living room, but he really loved them and made some elaborate setups. These were great fun for us to take command of, running multiple trains on multiple tracks at different speeds, with the living room lights turned down and the headlights piercing the night, running over bridges, through tunnels, and snaking up and over their own tracks. It was all great fun until one of the precarious little electric motors failed or some piece of rolling stock went missing. The man had a phenomenal mind for what belonged where and how many of each type of car or locomotive he had. I suspected that Mark had burnt out a motor or caused some other calamity with the steam engine that had mysteriously disappeared, and that he had stealthily ushered it back to his bedroom until he could figure out how to get it running again.

"What are you doing tomorrow?" Mark asked, directing the question to both of us.

"Not much—just playing with my stuff," Mike answered noncommittally.

"We're going to the Valley of the Fallen and El Escorial!" I announced, excited at the prospect.

It was our last day of vacation before heading back to school, and my dad had the day off. We'd been to both of these places, but it had been a few years since those trips. I think my parents sensed our boredom and figured it was time for a family outing. My sister wasn't so enthused—she wanted to spend the day with her friends at the teen club. After a few minutes of vigorous argument, she successfully made her case and was granted a day on her own. For my part, I couldn't wait to head out to the country with Mom and Dad to visit the giant cross on top of the mountain at the Valley of the Fallen.

My friends didn't seem all that interested in the trip.

"We went there once." Mark tossed the dice onto the game board.

"Was it cool?" Mike hadn't been in Spain long enough to get to all the monuments and historic towns around Madrid.

Mark shrugged and moved his piece. "It's really big."

The Valley of the Fallen was a stark, imposing monument to the men who had died during the Spanish Civil War, erected in their honor by Francisco Franco, the dictator who had led the Fascist forces during the war, and who had superseded the monarchy of Spain. Thirty-five years later, he was still in power, and his nation remained a quasi-military state.

My fascination with the history of Spain made me a bit of an outsider among my friends. I guess every young boy loves a castle, but a giant cross and a ceremonial crypt full of long-dead kings and fancy caskets? Maybe not so fascinating. My family tended to tour such places quite a lot. We went to most of them repeatedly. Once we toured the historic sites and cruised through the souvenir shops, we would, with great fanfare, spread our picnic blanket on a comfortable lawn or sit on a cool stone wall, looking out over a picturesque town clinging to a mountainside, a tumbling fortress crowning a steep escarpment, or a towering Gothic edifice with multiple spires reaching toward the sunny Spanish sky. It was our thing, and we had great fun with our picnics as we hauled from one medieval town to the next.

The following day, I waved to Mike, who was playing ping-pong with his father on his front porch. As we headed east, away from the city, the landscape offered an appearance far different from what I'd been used to in the Mid-Atlantic of the U.S., where I'd spent most of my life before we moved to Europe.

I pointed to a crumbling tower on a distant hill. "What do you think that was for?"

"There are so many castles around Madrid; they call this area of Spain, Castile." My mom always had an informative answer. "Probably a watchtower or the remnants of a much bigger castle."

The land was remarkable for the mesas—mountains with their tops worn off by water, wind, and time. Barren as they were, it was much easier to appreciate the skeletal appearance of the earth's craggy surface in that region than it had been when we were driving through the winding valleys of Western Maryland and the surrounding mountainous areas, looking up at the almost impenetrable thickets of deciduous trees and understory that carpet the rounded hills and mountains there. The Spanish hills reminded me of the stark vistas of the desert southwest in the U.S., which served as a backdrop for the cowboy films that enchanted young boys like me. I fantasized that our small company—Mike, Mark, and myself—with rifles slung over our shoulders, could scale the heights of one of the tall mesas in the distance, setting up an impenetrable strongpoint with command of the surrounding lowlands.

"Look, Dad, a C-5!" I suddenly called out from the back seat, pointing up at the low-flying, massive jet, its wings drooping low as it prepared to land at Torrejon.

"It's a big bird," he announced with tempered enthusiasm.

He worked at the base hospital, only a few hundred yards away from the flight line, so he saw all sorts of aircraft land and take off almost every day.

"How long till we get there?" I asked, looking out at the long line of flat-topped hills.

"We just started out," my mother said dryly. "We've got over an hour to go."

I sighed. It wasn't an ever-changing landscape. The novelty of observation wore off as the miles ticked away. I settled into my *GI Combat* comic books while we drove up to the mountains where the great cross stood.

As the drive wore on, I put down the comics and stared out the window. Mesmerized by the scenery rushing by, I thought about my circumstances. Life was changing for me, most conspicuously in my sister's gradual withdrawal from our family activities. We were natural rivals; I resented her age and privilege, while she was jealous of the attention my parents lavished on me, both as the youngest child and as the emerging scholar. My father, especially, had great respect for educational accomplishments. While stoic, he did not fail to praise me when I brought home a notable report card, which was happening more frequently with Mr. Walden as my teacher.

This distance between my sister and I had only increased over the past two years as she grew taller and matured into a young woman, spending more time primping and gossiping about boys. All I could see was the loss of what camaraderie we once had, for she had been closely aligned with me for years as a united front against parental oppression and a friendly combatant in our feet-to-feet battles in the back seat during long car rides.

I didn't often dwell upon the loss I was beginning to sense as she distanced herself from the family, growing closer to her peers. But for some reason, I felt it keenly that day. It could have been the somberness of the places we were visiting—a towering memorial to thousands of war dead and, later, a massive mausoleum erected centuries before as the resting place for Spanish kings and queens. Perhaps it was the gray sky that had gradually replaced the clear blue as we drove farther from Royal Oaks. Or perhaps it was simply the emotional letdown I could not ignore after the long-awaited Christmas season ended.

Kathy had a liveliness about her; she was observant and had a fine sense of humor, which made for an excellent back seat partner. I tried to comfort myself by noting that, with her at home, I had the entire back of the car to myself. I could stretch out, put my feet up, even lie down and sleep. But the other side of the back seat now felt awfully empty.

I couldn't help but contrast Kathy's approach to life with my own. She was entering the world as a young adult with a strong character and boldness. My father seldom spoke of it, but I knew he appreciated those aspects of her nature. I was astounded by her willingness to confront others and speak her mind. Once, when she was placed on a softball team that none of her friends played for, she pitched a complete fit until they put her on the Superbads, where her friend Karen had been placed. It must have been the right call, as they did win their league that year.

At any rate, I had my doubts whether I would have done the same. I was much more likely to accept what was thrust upon me.

"There it is," Dad called out sometime later as we rounded a curve. He'd caught sight of the great cross, which was still quite far away.

We fixed our eyes upon the scene as we drove on. The towering memorial had an imposing presence about it, and we remained silent as we approached, the cross growing ever taller in the frame of the windshield until it seemed impossibly large.

El Valle de los Caídos, the Valley of the Fallen, was awe-inspiring.

"How tall is it?" I could barely see the top of the magnificent cross.

"It's six hundred feet high, the pamphlet says." My mother read the statistics. She always had some literature to read to us.

We ambled to its base after parking the car, and I stood in the shadow of the monolith, tilting my head back so far it became almost painful. I didn't know how many people had died to sanctify that vast, monolithic emblem, but I knew it had been an awful lot.

"Thousands of people died in their civil war. It was a preamble to World War II, an early triumph for dictatorships. There is still great sorrow and bitterness among the Spanish people related to this war. This happened only about thirty-five years ago." I listened carefully as she summarized.

The war was recent enough that many of its veterans were still visible on the streets of Madrid. Bent and broken, stooped and disheveled, I would see them sitting on street corners or at small stands selling tickets for the national lottery. Many of them had lost arms or legs and spent the past few decades eking out a sparse living in state-sponsored employment. Apparently, this was the government's way of showing its appreciation for wounded veterans. We didn't buy lottery tickets—I don't think my father made enough to justify the waste. But when we walked past these men on the streets of Madrid, I felt a profound sense of sorrow for them—for their disabilities, for their stark existence, and for their meager position in society. In my innocence, I questioned the fairness of the world, which had demanded so much of these men, and rewarded them in such a paltry fashion.

"Dad, why did this war happen? Why did so many Spanish people fight against each other?"

I understood the basics of our U.S. Civil War, but not what happened in Spain.

"They disagreed about what type of government they should have. Some were in favor of keeping a king, some wanted socialism, others fought for the *Generalissimo*, who wanted to run the country himself, a dictator. The dictator won—he had some help from the forces of other dictators in Europe—and he's still here, in charge of the country."

"Seems like they could have figured all that out without killing so many people."

He nodded as we walked into the base of the great monument. "I think all wars are like that."

A sort of church, a basilica, had been built into the base of the mountain upon which the cross stood. A guide told us that prisoners of war, many of whom perished during construction, had hewn the rock using hand tools. The actual space within the mountain was glorious. The stone shone like polished alabaster. Floors, ceilings, columns, walls, altar: all were radiant. In the inner recesses were said to be the coffins of thousands of soldiers from both sides who had died in the bloody conflict, which had been a staging ground for the weaponry used to such fearsome effect a few years later, in World War II. The serenity within this capacious chamber was moving.

We walked through the sacred space with reverence, speaking little as we marveled at what had been accomplished inside the mountain, and only then in hushed tones. Even though we'd seen it before, it still awed us. The silence inside the basilica had swallowed up those touring it, as though it were a medium of its own, absorbing and oppressing any sound.

Our brief journey was steeped in solemnity and marked to some degree by mourning, even for those of us who had lost no one in the war that shattered the Iberian Peninsula. As we moved about beneath this towering symbol of destruction and sacrifice, the sadness and loss the nation had experienced so many years before were nearly palpable.

"Kathy would've been bored anyway." I put my hands in my pockets as we headed toward the car.

"What?" The mention of my sister caught my mother off guard.

"Kathy. I don't think she would have liked this trip."

"Well," she offered, "she's having more fun these days at the teen club with all her friends. That's part of growing up."

That didn't buoy my mood. The fragmentation of my family filled me with a strange anxiety. Maybe the melancholy surroundings we experienced that day were symbolic: the dissolution of a nation and of a family. How, I wondered, would I move forward on my own, as my sister, who had long been my protector and advocate, headed off into her own life?

She was changing—my whole family was changing—and so was I. On this gloomy day, emerging from this place of profound grief, it registered deeper within me, and it was unsettling. The sheltered, stable existence I'd enjoyed within my family for my entire young life was deteriorating.

The trip was not to become any more joyful. After leaving the Valley of the Fallen, we drove to the palace at El Escorial, the designated resting place for generations of Spanish kings and queens. The Escorial was an austere gray palace, over five hundred years old, nestled in the depths of a valley. Its sheer gray walls protruded from the surrounding forest—a massive, angular stone extending skyward from a restless green surf.

"Why did they bury all their kings and queens in one place?"

This seemed strange to me. Our presidents were usually laid to rest in their hometowns, among their loved ones.

"Kings and queens are different," my mom suggested. "They're almost like a part of the country itself, not elected leaders from among the people. The Spanish people were subjects of the royal leaders, but they also felt they owned the kings and queens, like they were part of the country's soul. They wanted to visit them after they died. This is a place to pay homage to hundreds of years of royalty. A source of national pride."

As soon as we entered the Escorial, we met a tour guide who directed us to the art museum inside the complex. Paintings of kings, queens, and religious figures that marked the art of the medieval period filled the museum. Most of these works of art depicted wan faces, notable for pious fervor or royal bearing. These were set upon black, foreboding backgrounds, as if life in those times was dark and joyless. Others portrayed Christ on the cross with variable techniques, each renowned for some aspect of light, color, tone, or perspective. Even with my rudimentary appreciation of art, I could see that these painters were masters at capturing the radiance of heaven as it shone down on the savior, whether he hung, dying, on the wooden cross or lay lifeless in the arms of Mary.

Although I had been baptized into the Catholic Church, and attended Catholic schools before I went to Spain, I seldom thought much of the crucifixion of Christ. The event was, to me, a symbol of faith, something before which to bow down or cross oneself, but little more than that. However, I could not help, as I looked at centuries of portrayals of this act of love and sacrifice, changing my perspective. The innumerable characterizations of Christ I saw during my time in Spain, in the museums, churches, and cathedrals, allowed me to see Him more plainly as a man, not solely a deity, who was tortured and killed by the brutal soldiers of an oppressive government. I wondered how He could have endured that gruesome ritual, to hang from a wooden frame with spikes placed through His limbs, observed by a crowd of amused spectators, as death came slowly. The great Spanish painters captured that scenario with stunning realism. I don't know if this newfound appreciation of Christ's sacrifice made me a better person, but it made me take my faith more seriously.

We moved on to a spacious hall filled with the coffins of the Spanish kings and queens, an image that characterized the Escorial. The final resting place for the regents was a huge circular stone chamber, with walls punctuated by rectangular recesses. Inside of these rested the oblong boxes, handsomely adorned with gold leaf and ornate script, identifying the royal denizen who lay within.

"It's kind of spooky, all these coffins in one room." A chill ran down my spine, and I tried to keep my voice down out of respect for the Spanish visitors, who felt a deep reverence for this place.

"These are great leaders of Spain, from many generations." My dad nodded solemnly. "This country, in its most powerful years, was the seat of an empire that controlled much of the world, and opened up an entire segment of the globe to exploration and colonization."

The car was quiet on the drive home, as we considered what we'd seen. And it may have made us all a bit more depressed that we were out sightseeing without my sister. Our small family had begun to splinter as she entered adolescence. That her friends were becoming more important to her than family would have seemed impossible even a year earlier. It didn't improve my mood much to consider that Christmas vacation was nearly at its end, and I'd soon have to return to school.

Nineteen

Monday, our first day back at school, was difficult and depressing. It was so natural and appropriate to be away from studies, and the winter holidays had been so joyful that returning to the classroom was an emotional letdown. Somehow, though, Gene C. Walden turned it around. He seemed so glad to see us, greeting virtually everyone in the class by name, laughing and joking.

"Steven, tell me about your Christmas!"

"Mauro, what did Santa bring you?"

"TC, what did your family do for the holidays?"

"Louis, do you miss Saigon this time of year?"

After he captured our attention, he opened a book to one of his favorite short stories. As I listened to Mr. Walden read "The Most Dangerous Game," I sensed a transformation coming over me. I am not sure why it struck me so forcefully at that moment. Surely, this had been occurring for months—not only for me but for many of the students fortunate enough to be in his room. He fostered a sense of intellectual curiosity and excitement about learning in me and many other students, even when he wasn't in our midst. Studying and learning what he presented and assigned had become a natural response: I wanted to know what he wanted me to know.

This new sense of scholarly responsibility and achievement would dramatically remake my self-impression. As a slight and introverted boy with no special athletic qualifications, I had previously harbored no illusions about my place in the great pyramid of society. In fact, given the opportunity, I would head directly for the lowest tier. But after a few months in Mr. Walden's classroom, I began to develop a sense of personal value.

When I had discovered the thrill of learning about human anatomy and announced to my father that I wanted to be a physician soon after moving to Spain, he was politely enthused. But he carefully explained how many years of study and toil this would require. He reminded me that no one in our family, on my mother's side or my father's, had ever been to college.

"This will be a pretty big step up for our family." Two years later, in the hands of this remarkable teacher, I began to believe that I could truly achieve this far-flung goal. Mr. Walden instilled a seed of self-esteem that had been lacking before he entered my life.

It was rapid fire in his classroom every day.

"Let's go over your book reports."

"I want to see some colorful pictures for your books."

"Let's look at some of the Spanish buildings we could draw for our posters."

"Fractions aren't hard. You just have to keep at them."

"Everyone stand up and stretch. I want to show you the steps to the Mexican hat dance!"

Mr. Walden also pushed us into places we were not comfortable, but which afforded the opportunity for growth. One bleak afternoon in late January, I was surprised when Mr. Walden called my name.

"Steven, can you come to the front of the class?"

He didn't sound angry, so I was puzzled.

"Everyone, I have an announcement. Each year, we choose a few students from the fifth-grade class to serve in the audio-visual club. For being prompt, hard-working, reliable, and enthusiastic, this serves to reward those we think will take great pleasure in assisting in our educational process."

I suddenly felt warm, and my face turned red.

"This year, I chose Steven to serve in this position. Let's give him a round of applause."

I looked down at my shoes and let a smile creep across my face. This was a high honor.

The next day, Mr. Jacobs, one of the fourth-grade teachers, who taught us science, brought me and the other selected students together to teach us the nuances of running the 32mm projectors and the simpler filmstrip machine.

"Be careful," Mr. Jacobs explained, adopting a serious expression. "If you don't get the filmstrip started just right, the machine will chew up the film, and it's almost impossible to correct the situation. It will keep feeding, destroying the filmstrip, and some sort of jumbled image will be projected. It's not pretty. When it feeds correctly, it's fine, and there's nothing else to do but push the button when the teacher says to advance the slide. But if you get started on the wrong foot, it's really a problem."

I envisioned this, looking through narrowed eyes at the filmstrip machine. It seemed complicated—how would I know the film was feeding incorrectly before it was too late to reverse it? No one else in the group asked any questions, and I assumed they all got it, so I should get it, too. I made a mental note to talk to Mr. Jacobs after the session.

"The 16mm projector seems much more complex, but it's actually pretty easy to get started," he explained to us, demonstrating how to feed the film. "It's less temperamental, and even if it misfeeds, it's easy to catch it right away and salvage things."

And then, very quickly, our instructional session was over. I forgot to catch up with Mr. Jacobs to ask about the filmstrip, but it seemed a distant and unlikely problem. And, as I expected, my first three or four requests to provide AV support in the school were for 16mm films. I felt pretty special, as I was the only one in my classroom selected for the AV club.

A few weeks later, a teacher asked me to set up a filmstrip for another class to help illustrate one of their history lessons. I was excused from my classroom and went to the supply closet to get the filmstrip machine. I felt a sense of foreboding as I opened the door and turned on the light. I had not bothered to clarify how I would know if the thing was misfeeding or how to abort the process before I destroyed the filmstrip. I anxiously regarded the little brown box, with its dark, round, shining lens projecting like a mischievous eye. Grabbing it, I hastened to the classroom and my destiny.

"Oh, there you are," Mrs. Allen said, with a broad smile and some degree of appreciation in her voice.

I'd been in her class the year before, and for all I knew, she'd supported the recommendation that I be included in the AV club. I nodded confidently to her and set to work with the machine and the filmstrip she handed me. She continued her lecture on the American Revolution while I put things together. My fingers began to shake as I turned on the machine and proceeded to feed the film. At first, it went without a hitch. She looked over at me, and I signaled that all was well.

"Now, everyone, one of my best students from last year, Steven, is going to run our filmstrip while I look over your essays."

She returned to her desk, dimmed the lights on the way, and sat down. Once I started with the filmstrip, she would put on a record that provided the audio, and the soundtrack would cue me on when to advance to the next image.

It was my show at that point. I pressed the button to advance the film and heard a not-so-reassuring crinkling sound as the strip fed into the maw of the little brown monster. I pressed the button again, hoping that advancing the film was a solution to the misfeed. It wasn't. The alarming sound became louder, and the filmstrip began to move awkwardly, taking a somewhat crooked pathway into the machine. Light shone from the lens, but the screen displayed only a curious image of multiple slides superimposed, one on the next, in an unintelligible mess. Perspiration collected on the back of my neck and in my armpits. Mrs. Allen was working on her papers, but the class was getting a bit restless, and I could hear hushed voices as the students began wondering aloud what was going on.

"What's he doing?"

"I can't see the pictures."

There was a smattering of laughter, and I began to feel frantic. Hitting the feed button again, I realized I had no real alternative maneuver. This time, there was a much louder crunching sound as the machine protested loudly. The loop of film doubled back on itself, bulging up out of the throat of what had become, in my mind, an uncontrollable beast, spitting out the tonic that I insisted it ingest.

Increasingly frustrated, I began to whisper to myself. "How do you *do* this?"

By this time, the teacher's attention had re-focused on me, and I could feel the hot light of discretion from everyone in the class. It wasn't where I wanted to be and was made far worse because of the praise she'd heaped upon me just minutes before, in front of a naive fourth-grade audience, which no doubt looked upon me as a capable, knowledgeable upper-classman. But I was powerless to troubleshoot the failed feed, wishing intently that I had stayed back in Mr. Walden's class that afternoon.

"Steve, what's wrong?" Mrs. Allen asked sympathetically, walking over to me.

My voice wavered as I tried to explain. "I can't get this to go through."

She looked at the crumpling film, bulging up out of the machine, which continued to complain loudly. "So I see. Don't worry, I'll call Mr. Jacobs."

She was not the least bit unkind or accusatory. Perhaps other fifth-grade AV boys had made a mess of things in her class on other occasions. She hurried to the door and disappeared for a moment that felt like a year. The students murmured loudly to each other while my cheeks burned red with embarrassment.

When she reappeared, with Mr. Jacobs in tow, I wasn't sure whether to be relieved or even more ashamed. But he was as kind and supportive as he had been when instructing us on the fine points of the machines.

"Here, Steve, let's see," he said warmly, examining the situation.

His self-assuredness rippled through me, soothing my shame. In short order, he had things running smoothly, and he had me continue at my post, running the strip to the soundtrack cues for the next half hour. I thanked the teacher respectfully and retreated, disgraced, to my homeroom.

I thought later about the episode and how Mr. Jacobs handled things. It was not clear to me whether having confidence simply made one's behaviors appear better in the eyes of onlookers, or if developing a certain level of self-regard somehow affected a person's judgment or actions so that things actually turned out in the desired way. I wished that I could somehow display such a characteristic. But it was not in me, at least not yet. And, I conceded, it couldn't simply be projected without the substance beneath. Either you had this confident nature, or you did not. Still, I hoped to someday acquire it.

I was too young at that point to appreciate that if you take on a challenge over and over again or if you repeatedly train to manage a difficult situation, it can eventually lead to real confidence.

Life had many lessons waiting for me.

Twenty

"Don't be afraid of the ball, Steve! Step forward, keep your eye on it, and make contact. You've done this at home a hundred times. It's no different here. Just be aggressive."

It was late winter, and time for the annual tryouts for Little League baseball in Royal Oaks. Right after the hitting session, Dad had taken me aside for a bit of a pep talk. I had fouled off a few pitches, swung at a bunch more, and managed to hit a couple of grounders into fair territory.

His blue eyes sparkled with an intensity I knew was not evident in my own. I watched the other boys, some of whom really *were* aggressive, rushing up to grounders, swinging the bat with authority, and bearing down on their fastballs with all the strength they could summon while pitching.

I would have been content to let the tryouts slip by altogether, since I was planning an active lizard-hunting campaign for the spring with my friends. Unfortunately, Mark and Mike both played baseball, and my father was too well informed to forget the date. So, I ended up in the gym on a cool February Saturday, reluctant and a little anxious. A hall full of competitive boys, each intent on impressing the coaches and outdoing the next guy, was not a place I really wanted to be. It was a show-off session, as intended, and I was not good at that. With eight other boys on the field, I could remain quiet and unnoticed, at least most of the time. But in the gym, I was performing for keen, judgmental eyes. And I almost always managed to underperform.

My problematic self-doubt was most evident when I played baseball, which required split-second decision-making, hand-eye coordination, and rapid application of skills in a demanding set of circumstances. I knew my reluctance was painfully visible on the baseball diamond. The outfield was the repository for unskilled players in Little League, since small boys could seldom hit the ball that far, and I was consigned to play in right field for most of the games.

In this arena, my father was determined to help me find inner strength, and he expended much time and effort in his tutelage. It was a personal slight to him when I danced out of the way of a ground ball, twisted my glove in some awkward fashion as a line drive ball approached, or turned my head away from a ball rapidly approaching me, whether off a bat or out of someone's throwing hand. My timid nature was evident in the way that I approached every aspect of the game, from hitting to fielding to base-running. And though I fantasized about being a pitcher while throwing the ball with my dad in our yard, my coaches hadn't seen that potential.

"OK, where are my outfielders? Everybody line up at the far end of the gym. I'm gonna hit you some soft liners. One at a time, when you throw the ball in, just circle back and get in line again. Got it?"

One of the coaches herded us along, indicating where we would form up together. I fell in at the end of the line, shifting my weight from leg to leg while the other boys hustled after the rubber-coated baseballs that kept coming our way.

Finally, it was time to demonstrate my fielding skills. I watched nervously as Mr. Marlow tossed the ball up and swung, sending a well-placed line drive in my direction. It was one of those hits that made you freeze—if I moved up, I doubted I could catch it and would likely be subjected to a "short hop" at my feet; if I moved back, it might bounce hard off the gym floor and go over my head. I found my feet and quickly took two steps back. The ball predictably careened off the wooden surface. It sprang over my head into the bleachers behind me, where my father sat.

Dad tossed the ball to me, his face registering one of those expressions that showed I'd not quite met his expectations.

Coach Marlow spoke to the group, as I'd provided a favorable teaching moment. "You've got to break on that ball the second it leaves the bat. If you wait, you're gonna miss it."

I rejoined the line of outfielders, chatting happily amongst themselves, intent on proving their abilities. I tried to melt in, to fade from sight, but I could feel all those eyes on the other side of the gym boring into me, ranking me against the others.

Dad desperately wanted me to be as assertive and skilled as he was on the field. But I wasn't. I tried, but I feared failure, which often paralyzed me. I thought more about striking out than I did about hitting the ball. I cared more about missing the pop fly than I did about getting the batter out. And I don't know which I dreaded most: being inept on the diamond or disappointing my father. Playing baseball was not as rewarding as it should have been for a boy my age.

Just two years before, Dad had formally introduced me to baseball, a step up from the Wiffle ball I had enjoyed as a young boy in Cumberland. I was so reluctant and so intimidated by the hardball that it nearly drove him crazy. He gave me a lot of encouragement, and he was patient enough to go over the fundamentals repeatedly. I got some of it. I wasn't a terrible fielder, though I always waited for the ball to come to me—I was never bold enough to go tearing after it. If it was coming to me, I reasoned, why should I rush up to it, especially if it might take an unpredictable bounce?

But hitting was something else. I couldn't manage to bring the bat to the ball. I diligently followed Dad's instructions: bat back over my shoulder, front elbow up, eyes on the ball, feet square to the plate, swing through the approaching ball. It was all to no avail.

I had played my first season for a team called the Tigers, with Jeffrey Marlow's father as coach and a very kind man named Mr. Leonetti as assistant coach. I played in the outfield, and I was clearly a weak link. There were twenty games, and through the first sixteen, I didn't get a single hit. But I did get a lot of encouragement.

"Steve, you're doing everything right," my dad had confided one day as we drove home from a game in the Peugeot. "Eventually, the law of averages has got to give you a hit."

That sounded good to me. I didn't understand the "law of averages," but if it would award me a successful trip along the base paths, I was all for that.

Once, as the team huddled after a game to discuss how things had gone, Mr. Leonetti talked about ways to improve our hitting. He shocked me by holding me up as an example.

"Take Stevie, here. He hasn't hit it yet, but he's got the best swing on the team. When he connects . . . Pow! It's gonna fly."

I was elated by the compliment and shared it with my dad, who enthusiastically agreed.

As fate would have it, during the very next game, the law of averages finally paid me the predicted visit, and I connected with the ball—a double! Well, to be more accurate, it was a single with a bad throw from the outfielder, but for me, it was an earned trip to second base. A long time in coming, this first hit was followed by a bloop single on the next at-bat. From first base, I looked at my father, who, in his taciturn way, was nodding his approval with just a hint of satisfaction registered on his features. If I had smiled any more broadly as I arrived safely at second after the next boy up smacked the ball, I might have permanently injured my face.

"Yay, Steven!" Mrs. Reimolds, who often came to see me play, clapped and cheered. I could hear how delighted she was, and her enthusiasm spread throughout the small crowd in the bleachers. Warmth spread through me; I was certain I had become privy to some universal secret, that the key to athletic success had finally been delivered to me. And it felt beautiful indeed.

When we drove home that afternoon, I sat up front with my dad. I was especially proud to sit beside him.

"You see? If you keep doing things the right way, and you go after the ball, you're going to hit it. It's not that hard," he told me, clearly pleased with himself for helping me attain success at last.

I was anxious for the next game so that I could redouble my efforts and capitalize on my success, cranking out more hits. I did manage to beat out the throw after I hit a grounder to the shortstop, mainly because the guy bobbled the ball. But after that, the law of averages moved on to some other deserving character. I had no more hits for the rest of the year, though Mr. Leonetti continued to praise my swing as it was level and forceful.

One day after school in February, about a week after tryouts, I joined up with Mike as we walked home.

"Did you find out which team you're gonna be on?" Mike was excited about the team that had picked him.

"Yeah," I answered. "The Toros. They won the championship last year, so I think we'll be pretty good. I hope I can play good enough to be on the starting team."

"You worry too much," Mike assured me. "What are you going out for?"

"Outfield. Just outfield."

"I thought you were pitching? I see you in your yard, pitching to your dad all the time."

"Well, we have some really good pitchers. You know that guy Stocker is on the Toros, right? So I don't think I'd get to pitch, anyway."

Stocker threw the ball hard and accurately. He was so good that all the other kids just referred to him by his last name, an honor in our circle. I was secretly thankful I would not have to be in the batter's box when he was on the mound. Though I harbored my fantasies about pitching, and I practiced with my father when we were at home together, I declined his urgings that I try out for the position. There could be no more visible person on the entire diamond than the pitcher, and I wasn't quite ready for that. If there weren't enough pitchers on our team, or if someone had to miss a game, I figured the coach might call me to the mound, especially if I showed some ability during our practices. And I was content to leave it at that.

"How about you?" I wondered which team had grabbed Mike.

"I'm on the Pegasos. I think we're gonna be really good this year." My friend's confidence showed through, as it usually did. "Did you hear anything about Mark?" he asked, practicing his swing.

"He found out yesterday. He's on the Aguilas. You know, the Eagles." I'd had more exposure to Spanish than Mike, so I liked to translate for him.

"I heard they're not so good."

"Me too. But Mark's a year older than most of them, so he should get to play a lot."

It would be another month before practice began in earnest. But I knew the three of us would get together with ball and gloves when we could and practice on our own once the weather improved.

Winter, or what passed for it, was a pretty brief season in Madrid. The short, cool days began to lengthen, and the afternoons became warm and sunny. I sensed the call of the gullies, and I yearned to go back to hunting for our newly emerged quarry. Sometimes, it seemed like there were too many things to do in Royal Oaks—practicing baseball, hunting for lizards, playing army, tossing gliders and parachute men off the terraza. We simply couldn't pack it all in after school on weekdays. But it was a wonderful problem to have, in a wonderful place.

Twenty-One

My friendships with Mark and Mike weren't without hiccups. We were forever triangulating, two against one, for trivial reasons. We'd argue about the meaning of a word, or pronunciation, or something we'd seen in a film. One day, while walking down to baseball practice after school, Mark confronted me about a horror movie that had recently come to our theater on Royal Oaks.

"You and Mike went to see that scary movie, right?"

"*The Abominable Dr. Phibes.* Yeah. It was pretty spooky. I couldn't watch some parts of it. I put my head down under the seats."

"I thought we were all gonna go and see it together?" It was clear Mark was peeved.

"Well, you said you couldn't go. You had practice. So we went ourselves."

"Why didn't you wait for me? I could've gone on Friday."

"I know. But the movie was supposed to change on Friday. That's why we went."

He said nothing more about it, but I knew it would be a sore point for a while.

A few days later, Mike and I dropped by to see Mrs. Reimolds, who offered us lemon-lime popsicles. She noticed there were only two of us.

"Where's Mark today?" she asked.

We looked at each other awkwardly.

"Oh, I see. You boys are having words?"

It was the gentlest way to put it, precisely the way I thought she would characterize such things. Especially compared to my mother, who could turn into a fireball in an instant. It was hard to imagine Mrs. Reimolds being in an argument or even being angry. TC assured me that she had her moments, but I was doubtful.

I dropped over to see Mrs. Reimolds the following week, Mark at my side, but Mike wasn't with us. She didn't ask. We did seem to turn on each other at a moment's notice, but to our credit, we would put things back together again in short order. Those episodes often helped me to look at the other guys' perspectives and maybe even taught me to be a more loyal friend. Sometimes I was the one on the outs, and it was painful. When it happened, I thought about my behavior and how I'd contributed to the disagreement. At first, I would feel resentful and bitter toward the other two, wondering how they could exclude me, and a sort of angry paranoia coursed through me. But as I considered my own words and actions, it wasn't always clear that I was the virtuous one, and I looked forward to making up with them.

Even so, our sometimes-awkward, three-way friendship had a lynchpin. Adventures in the gullies allowed us to bury our conflicts and accept each other again, playing to our common interests. This shared value—the appreciation of our little reptilian friends—could bring us together no matter how far our foolish attitudes and petty spats drove us apart. It was common for a pair of us, who were getting along well at the moment, to head down into those badlands and start prowling around, searching for our elusive quarry, only to have the sullen outsider come down as well and join the hunt. And we'd be off again on a new expedition, the cross feelings and angry words of the prior day forgotten.

On an afternoon in early spring, Mike and I sat together on his patio, chatting and playing a board game. We often played games or ping-pong there until we became bored or restless.

"It's your turn," I said to Mike, who was distracted from the game arrayed on the table in front of us.

"Let's go down to the gullies," he suggested, throwing the dice.

"But I'm winning," I protested.

"OK. Five more minutes, then we go." Mike figured he would pull it out before we abandoned the game. It was a sunny, warm Saturday, and we'd both had baseball practice in the morning. I threw a couple of unfortunate rolls of the dice, and Mike passed me up. On his next turn, he rolled precisely what he needed to win.

"So, cut low," he said, smiling impishly.

It was the standard expression to express momentary superiority among the kids in Royal Oaks. The phrase was usually accompanied by a flat-handed flick of the wrist to simulate figurative slicing and dicing.

I wasn't always the most gracious loser, especially when victory had been snatched away unexpectedly. I had to find a way to compensate for my humiliation. "Well—I'll race ya!"

I scampered out of my seat, around the corner, and out the gate, with Mike's dog, Frenchie, snapping at my heels.

Mike was a bit stockier than me and not quite as quick. Plus, he had a late start. He followed dutifully, with no recourse but to respond to my challenge. I disappeared over the hill, across Mark's driveway, and down into the most sizable trench in the maze of gullies. Weaving my way along the bottom, I turned a corner into a smaller, intersecting ditch, the sandy soil spraying up beneath my sneakers. As I cut to change direction, my eyes fixed on something in front of me that stopped me dead in my tracks. Perched on the edge of the gully, just outside the shelter of a sage bush, was a smallish lizard, frozen in its surprise and fear, watching me intently. He was perhaps six inches long, with the tail making up over half the length, dark in color, almost black, with fine golden pinstripes running his entire length.

I tried to catch my breath, holding as still as possible, admiring the small reptile.

At long last, I was staring at a six-lined racerunner for certain. There was no doubt about this sighting.

I heard a clatter behind me, then Mike's panting. I held my hand up in the air and tried to emphasize that I was on to something that demanded a stealthy approach.

"What is it?" he whispered over my shoulder.

I pointed.

"Wow, cool. What kind is it?" my friend asked, truly fascinated.

I motioned him closer. The lizard tilted his head, watching us closely but staying put.

"Look at the stripes," I breathed.

Suddenly, another voice called out from up on the edge of the trench behind us.

"Hey, what are you guys doing?"

I turned and glared at Mark as he approached. He took the hint. Nothing but a significant lizard sighting would have made me act this way. Turning about, he stealthily tiptoed along the gully, circling behind our quarry. Mike and I simply admired the diminutive reptile, which fixed its tiny black eyes on us warily. I knew he would be gone the moment he sensed a real threat. We had an opportunity to catch the most desirable and elusive of lizards, and Mark had come in at exactly the right moment. If my friend could get close enough, he would take the lizard entirely by surprise, flushing him away from his hole, which surely lay under the sage bush behind him. I figured that the little creature would then likely flee in our direction.

Lying in wait with four hands and four feet to create a barrier, we had a decent chance to corner him. It would be the crowning achievement of three years of reptilian pursuit, a real prize. I knew other boys who professed to be as interested in lizards as we were, but none who'd ever caught a six-lined racerunner. Some doubted that they even existed where we lived. I was hungry for the triumph of bagging the fastest land animal around and for bragging rights in Royal Oaks.

After a few seconds, Mark approached from behind the spindly shrub as stealthily as he could manage. Mike and I stood stock-still, setting ourselves for the inevitable scamper down into the gully and, hopefully, into our waiting hands.

I heard the snap of a twig, saw Mark's eyes startle with surprise, and the lizard cocked his head in that direction. Our friend then lurched forward, purposely stomping clumsily and making as much noise as a seventy-pound boy can make in the dry brush and fallen leaves. Right on cue, the lizard broke over the edge of the ditch, a streamlined blur, and then darted between my feet in an instant. We'd barely had time to bend over when we found he was already behind us, up the other bank, disappearing beneath some vegetation. I looked up at Mark, then at Mike, eyes wide.

"Wooow!"

"I guess," Mike offered, "that's why they call them racerunners."

I just shook my head.

"Maybe, just maybe, we met our match." Mark was a bit discouraged.

I considered the situation. At least we now knew where one of these guys lived. And we understood how incredibly fast he was. "Well, we'll need a new strategy."

"Like what? Get six more people to surround him?" Mike had a good point and took no pains to hide his skepticism.

"I don't know. I'll have to think about it," I admitted. There had to be a way to catch this marvelous little lizard.

"We'll have to stake him out and figure out the best way to be ready when he tries to escape."

Mark looked frustrated. "I thought you guys were ready!"

"Yeah, we thought so, too."

At least the sighting of the six-lined racerunner had brought all three of us together for a common purpose after weeks of skirmishing and taking potshots at one another. Our arguments now seemed trivial compared to the thrill of successfully catching this little guy. With baseball practices and games on weeknights and weekends, it would be harder to get the three of us together at the same time. But we were determined, and our little band vowed to keep up the vigorous pursuit.

Twenty-Two

There was an excitement that baseball season brought with it—the school year was getting on, and there was an end in sight. It was already late March, and we were counting the weeks until summer vacation. I had been looking forward to April for some time since my Uncle Bill and Aunt Connie were coming to visit us for two whole weeks. My parents had planned a trip to the south of Spain so that we could tour the fabled city of Granada. I'd heard about the famed Moorish fortress there, the Alhambra, from our Spanish teachers, and other families had reported to us that it was a great location to visit.

"Dad," I asked, anticipating their arrival, "why do you tell your friends that Uncle Bill is a cool cat?"

It wasn't an expression I heard him use very often.

"Well, he was kind of the standout in your mother's family. He had a talent, then he went on to trade school to develop it, and later he started a successful business. After that, he bought himself a neat little Thunderbird to impress the girls . . . and married into one of the most prominent Italian families in Pittsburgh. That's all pretty cool stuff."

It sounded cool to me.

"Oh, and he wears those dark shades wherever he goes. And looks good doing it. Not everyone can pull that off."

My uncle brimmed with confidence, seemed to have the world on a string, and wore his success on his sleeve, as did his dark, pretty,

Italian wife. Her family owned property and restaurants in downtown Pittsburgh. The only boy in my mother's family, Uncle Bill had achieved his success after studying drafting and eventually starting a commercial art firm. He didn't even finish high school—he left early to attend a technical school.

Uncle Bill and Aunt Connie did not have children, something we whispered about, but the actual reason for this was uncertain. Of course, he was the apple of his mother's and stepfather's eyes, and they never lost an opportunity to apprise us of his latest adventures or acquisitions. Compared to my parents, Uncle Bill seemed daring, bold, and flashy; Kathy and I were fond of him. My sister had been on the receiving end of numerous pieces of jewelry, containers of makeup, and articles of colorful fashionwear from Aunt Connie, so her affection and admiration for my aunt came quite naturally.

"Hi, Uncle Bill! Hi, Aunt Connie!"

Our whole family went to Barajas Airport to greet them. I ran up the ramp, brimming with enthusiasm. My uncle shook my hand in a manly fashion. Aunt Connie looked a little feeble after the long flight, but she gave me a tepid hug.

We were thrilled to see our uncle, who was basically unflappable, and appeared to be stepping off a one-hour flight to Philadelphia. Aunt Connie looked wrung out, and confessed that the trip was tougher on her. She'd never flown such a long way before, and the jetlag was already weighing her down. I think we soon cheered her up with questions about home and with our stories of life in Royal Oaks. Over the next couple of days, we provided perspectives about our exciting life in Spain and chatted enthusiastically about the adventures we were sure to have with them.

Around the table, Uncle Bill regaled us with descriptions of his art and design accomplishments.

"When I was in tenth grade, I made a replica of Fort Duquesne out of popsicle sticks," he said, tracing the design on the tablecloth. Everyone familiar with Pittsburgh knew that the French log fort had been constructed in the shape of a pentagon and stood at "The Point" where the Monongahela and Allegheny rivers came together to create the mighty Ohio.

I was amazed at his feat of ingenuity and miniaturization.

"How did you know how to put them together?" I asked, trying to imagine this vast diorama.

"I had a plan of the fort—it was just a matter of laying out the outer walls, and then assembling the buildings inside. I think it took me over a month. But I won a blue ribbon in our history fair for that one." He spoke of all this casually, taking a sip of beer, but I could tell he was proud.

The next day, the five of us crammed into our Peugeot, leaving Kathy to stay with Anna-Marie since it was too difficult for her to miss an entire week of high school.

"We'll miss you," I called as we rolled out of the driveway.

Standing on the carport with her friend, she waved but did not look particularly distressed.

The trip down to southern Spain passed quickly as we peppered my aunt and uncle with questions.

"How is the city faring? We hear about work stoppages and strikes sometimes." Dad paid a lot of attention to the business news.

"It's Pittsburgh. Nothing changes. The steelworkers are endlessly at odds with the management. Most of the mills look like they're decaying and about to collapse. Al gets laid off every few months, then they call him back. It's a bad business—can't imagine what the future is. Just like that shit with the railroads ten years ago. Sorry, Stevie. Glad I run my own affairs." He continued, more enthused. "Con's family is tearing it up. The Pilot House is doing great. You can't get a reservation there on the weekend. Lucky we have an in. Her brothers sold some parking lots and made a killing."

It was all success, all the time.

In a few hours, we were ascending the mountains of southeastern Spain. Granada was a thrilling, unique city. It was as unlike Madrid as Sevilla but had a different feel. Many homes and businesses were situated on tall hills, as the city was in the foothills of the Sierra Nevada Mountains.

"That's it! That's the Alhambra!" I pointed at the fabled edifice, almost leaping out of my seat.

Crowning one of the hills in the city's center was the series of walls that ringed the Alhambra. It was both a fortress and a palace, the focal point of the late Moorish presence in Spain. Granada had been a world-renowned city at the height of the Moors' power and affluence. I craned my neck to see as much of it as possible as we drove along the avenue toward our hotel.

"Time for a siesta," my father said with some satisfaction as we settled into our hotel room. He'd earned a nap, having driven the eight hours with just one short stop. My mom concurred, and the two of them lay down.

I snuck past them, out onto the balcony, chuckling softly. My father had a curious habit of folding his hands on his belly when he napped, like a man in a casket at a viewing. We all laughed at him for that, but I think it was his position of optimum repose.

"Let's get out there!" I exclaimed once everyone had rested.

We set out on a walking tour with my aunt and uncle, trying to get a feel for the city before we began our sightseeing forays the next days. Unfortunately, Aunt Connie kept falling behind.

"I didn't think we'd be walking this far." She was limping a bit, and I noticed that her beautiful shoes, with high spiked heels, looked uncomfortable.

My family considered ourselves energetic tourists, and having to stop to rest every few blocks cramped our style. We finally picked a place to have dinner, a little restaurant with starched white tablecloths and plenty of attentive waiters.

"Hmmm . . . Not much here you like, Con-con?" Uncle Bill spent a lot of energy ensuring my aunt was satisfied.

We were surprised she found so little appeal in the food of southern Spain. Given her strong Italian roots, we figured she would love the fresh seafood, the preponderance of garlic in every dish, and the crusty bread.

"Maybe she doesn't like the olive oil," I suggested later to my parents. "You know, like Kathy and me—we didn't like the food here for a long time."

My father laughed. "That's hard to imagine. Italians are practically weaned on olive oil."

We emerged from the restaurant and went window shopping along the quaint streets. The *paseo* had just begun, the time of the evening when the city's denizens all came out to walk the streets. Streams of people marched along the sidewalks, families greeting families, children hand-in-hand, scurrying along to keep up with their parents. It was a ritual, engrained within the population over many generations, a means of getting exercise, socializing, taking the fresh air, and enjoying the splendid sights of their city. Uncle Bill was taken aback.

"They all come out and walk like this every day?" he asked.

"They do, Bill," my mom answered, always enthused to explain the Spanish customs. "It's the same in Madrid. The shops close up, people join their families, and they all walk around for an hour. Then they start heading out for dinner, or maybe cook at home. I think it gives them a good appetite."

"They do know how to have a good time," my uncle observed, enjoying the spectacle.

My dad concurred. "They don't seem to work quite so hard over here. Pretty much anything that needs to get done can get done manana."

Uncle Bill nodded, interpreting the word's meaning, even though he didn't speak any Spanish. The word for "tomorrow" was the same as the word for "morning." But Spaniards never said "good morning." They always said "good day." I figured that had something to do with not getting things done right away. My dad once laughed aloud when I'd explained my reasoning, but he didn't have a better explanation.

We walked up the steps to the hotel lobby and rode the ancient elevator to our rooms. Aunt Connie looked a little nervous as we pulled the metal grate across the open doorway, and the car began to move upward with a series of jerky motions.

"Relax, Con," Uncle Bill said reassuringly as he took a puff of his cigarette. "This thing has probably been doing the same thing for a hundred years."

We were all tired by this time and made an early night of it. As I got ready to lie down, I looked out the door across our small balcony, where I could see the Alhambra sprawling atop the rise, its walls illuminated in a warm, enticing glow. I couldn't wait to get there in the morning.

We set out early the next day, and as we approached the great fortress, I just had to run up the hill: gardens, fountains, an incomparable view over the city and the distant mountains . . . I was thrilled.

"Wait up, Stevie! We'll get there!"

I sensed that my uncle was almost as excited as me. Even Aunt Connie was moving briskly along the stone footpaths, though I noticed her shoes were not quite as tall as the ones from the day before.

The splendor of the Alhambra was immediately apparent when you approached it; the grand palace was almost intoxicating. The intensifying sunshine found its way into the many cool, open halls defined by the graceful arches of Moorish architecture. There were doorways or passages to the outside, from which courtyards beckoned and long, colorful drapes tossed in the warm breezes. The myriad archways ensured that ample light flooded the various chambers, which were cheerful and inviting. The rooms were barely furnished, their former occupants preferring openness to opulent displays of finery.

As we moved throughout the palace, the guide frequently led us outside onto tiled courtyards.

"The Moors came from a land where water was very sparse, and they cherished it. Water played a central role in almost every courtyard, throughout the gardens, and even in some of the inner rooms. You will see fountains, pools, rivulets, and tiny streams," explained our Spanish guide with polished English.

We followed him onto a large square courtyard, at the center of which was a ring of stone lions surrounding an elevated basin. Streams of water arched down into the pool at the base of the statues. This outdoor space, the Court of the Lions, was famous. I imagined the sultan lounging beside the cool water, fanned by servants and surrounded by the lovely young women of his harem, their faces covered by veils. It was as easy to conceive of such a scene here as it was to envision knights in dented armor moving about the battlements of the Spanish castles, furiously preparing for an armed onslaught.

Shortly after that, we went outside to explore the walled areas around the palace. Exotic plants and formal displays of fragrant little boxwood shrubs defined the gardens. There were neat lines of rose bushes, blooming in an array of beautiful colors, sharing their sweet scent on the wind.

"How would you dig coming out here every day to take your afternoon stroll?" my uncle pondered, peering at the vegetation around us over the rim of his dark glasses.

From the gardens that sprawled around the palace, there was a pathway up to an even higher level, a place called the Generalife, which was a breezy, cottage-like building that served as a sort of mini-palace that the sultans had once used to escape the frustrations of life in the busy court. It, too, had a set of gardens around it.

I led the adults up, striding alongside a stone sluice carrying water down from the highest levels.

"See those mountains?" My mother pointed to the snow-covered peaks of the Sierra Nevada to the south of us.

"The snowmelt from those mountains is piped here to the Alhambra. The Moors captured that water and channeled it to this hilltop. It makes its way from the top, through all these little troughs and ponds in the gardens, down to the palace, where it fills the fountains and pools. Then it runs down to the river at the base of the hill."

"Well, these cats certainly knew how to live, didn't they?" My uncle adjusted his sunglasses and lit a cigarette while we rested on a bench.

I liked to sit beside him. Somehow his devil-may-care, brassy approach to life, so different from my own hesitation, attracted me. I thought that someday I'd like to be like him: accomplished, admired, unphased by the relentless flow of challenges life brought.

I stretched my legs out in front of me in the bright sunshine and then froze. A lizard lay motionless on a rock not far from where we sat. It was smallish, perhaps four inches long, probably on the young side. Both he and I remained completely still, intent upon one another. At least I thought he was eyeing me, for his gaze was intent upon something in my direction.

I carefully measured the distance between us in my mind and figured I could cover it in two steps. Tensing every muscle, I prepared to spring upon my wary little friend while my aunt continued to talk. Our mellow chatter provided the cover I needed, encouraging the lizard to keep sunning himself. I leaped toward him in a flash, startling the others on the bench and catching the frightened animal by surprise.

And with virtually no protest, he was in my hand.

I paraded him around for everyone to see. He was a brownie, all right, but his markings were a bit different than what we were used to seeing at home.

"Now that is a handsome lizard," Uncle Bill observed.

Aunt Connie was ill at ease but agreed that he was a looker.

"Okay, okay, now it's time to set him free," my father suggested. I looked the lizard over one last time, satisfied that I'd captured him. But I was not quite ready to give him up to the garden.

"See you, little guy." I placed him, gently but reluctantly, under some boxwood shrubs. In a moment, he was gone.

The afternoon was warm, breezy, and pleasurable. We glided through the gardens and courtyards, admiring all aspects of the Alhambra. It was impossible not to feel enchanted there. With the Generalife above us, the lofty white mountaintops on the distant horizon, and Granada spread out at our feet, I felt we were suspended in some celestial plane.

After a few days in Granada, we headed back to Madrid, though our visitors would stay with us for a few more days. My father and Uncle Bill sipped beer as we talked around the supper table each night. I liked to hear his stories about his boyhood in Pittsburgh, and the Connelley Technical Institute, where he learned his trade.

"Uncle Bill, how did you get through such tough times and still make things work out? Mom says you had to go to an orphanage, and then the family lived in the projects."

At my age, I felt I could talk to him frankly about what he had been through.

He tipped his chair back and sipped his glass of San Miguel. "We had some tough times. I don't remember when we lived with my dad. But I remember when my mother lost it . . . too many things went wrong at once. She had four kids to raise, no husband, no job. She had to go into a rest home, or something like that. She kept Babe, but your mother, Chris, and I went into a Catholic orphanage. Some of the nuns were angels and some from hell. We were just kids . . . Chris and I wet the bed on our first night there. They made us stand in the hallway with our dirty sheets while the other kids filed past. I remember the humiliation. Chris just cried. You never forget something like that. One time, after they put us to bed and it was still light, Chris got out of her bed to look out the window. The nun came around, checking the rooms, and she caught her. She beat the shit out of that girl. I was terrified, and I pulled my covers over my head. I didn't know what to do. That was a really miserable time for us."

"When you got out, where did you go?"

"Mum came out of the home, and she got a job cooking with a church school, in Oakland over by St. Agnes. Your mom got a job in the same kitchen, cleaning up after school. We moved into the projects up on Allequippa Street. They weren't very nice houses—they're still there, behind Presbyterian Hospital, up on Cardiac Hill."

"Was it hard going to school, you know, without a dad?"

He shrugged. "A lot of the kids living there didn't have a dad. It was a tough neighborhood. There were a lot of fights. I went to school, but I didn't finish. I wanted to learn drafting and drawing, so I left school and went to Connelley, a trade school. I went back later and got my GED."

He seemed proud of that. I wondered how he had come through such tough times so successfully. He had not had a father for much of his life, and the time in the orphanage sounded truly awful. Others scorned the family in the public housing projects where they lived before my step-grandfather came along. A fatherless family on welfare attracted little respect. The neighborhoods were hardscrabble, and the kids around them were tough. Despite all that, Uncle Bill had found his calling, applied himself, and achieved what no one else in our family had. Many forces had aligned against him, but somehow, Uncle Bill overcame them.

My admiration for my uncle grew substantially during that trip. Always effervescent, he radiated confidence and a certain zeal for life and adventure, with his mate poised beside him, ready for the next chapter in their exciting existence. They were a sophisticated and fashionable couple, more cultured than anyone else I knew.

I was beginning to notice, as I approached the end of my elementary school years, how people made their way in the world and created conditions that allowed them to succeed. Uncle Bill reminded me of Mr. Jacobs, of Mr. Mazza, and in some ways of my friend Mike. There was something magical about the self-confidence all of them displayed. It seemed to pave the way for their accomplishments. And, as reticent as I was, I yearned to be successful someday, too.

Twenty-Three

Just a few days after my aunt and uncle left to return to the U.S., I went to baseball practice after school and had to walk home alone since my friends' practice sessions had finished earlier than mine. I ambled jauntily along the road, wondering if there would be time to play with Mike and launch some of our balsa gliders when I got home. Just as I was about to turn onto the path that led up through the gullies, I heard a voice.

"Hey, little guy, what are you doing?"

An older boy about my sister's age had come up quickly behind me. He was holding a sack, looking at me as though I were a mark. His manner was threatening, and I looked around me. There was not another person in sight, and I didn't think I could outrun him. I didn't reply.

"Here." He thrust the bag into my arms. Surprised, I wrapped my arms around it, shaking.

I could feel my face burning with shame. Accepting the package as a servant might receive a burden from his master, I did not speak.

"You can carry my milk. That way," he directed, pointing along the road and away from my path.

I put my head down and shuffled along, with him right behind me, jeering at me.

"We have to keep little people like you in line. Don't even think of running. I'll catch you, and I'll beat your ass."

I swallowed hard. I had seen him before, but I didn't know who he was or where he lived. It might be a long walk, I conceded to myself. There must have been something about me that made guys like that single me out for humiliation. It must have been clear that I would fall in line with their demands without much of a fight.

We walked along for a few minutes in silence. His footsteps sounded behind me, but I was afraid to turn around and look at him.

I was startled to see the Peugeot suddenly drive up and stop beside us. My father got out with as stern a look on his face as I had ever seen. For his part, my antagonist grabbed the milk and lit out through a front yard toward the back of a house I doubted was his. My father gave no chase, yelled no invectives, and paid little heed to the teenager.

Instead, he glared at me. I felt the sting of humiliation and tried to avoid the inevitable appearance of tears in my eyes, waiting for him to vent his anger. He had little tolerance for the pacific aspects of my nature, which he regarded as pure cowardice.

"Was that guy making you carry his bag?" he asked, chewing on the words and spitting them out like nails.

I could not hide from my father's angry stare. Every time I looked up, I had to put my head down again.

"Steve, you have to fight your battles. Who was that kid? Do you know him?"

I shook my head and felt a teardrop careen downward off the tip of my nose. At that, his demeanor softened, at least a bit.

"How could you let someone treat you like that? What did he say? Why didn't you just drop it on the ground? Or run away?"

I had no words to offer in my defense. I knew he was right. A profound sadness welled up inside of me: sadness because I was afraid, sadness because I'd let my father down, and sadness because I couldn't be something he wanted me to be.

"Promise me, next time you won't carry someone else's milk. You've got to be a man, Steve. You're growing up. I can't fight for you. If I had done what I wanted to do to him, I'd go to jail. *You* have to find the courage to stand up to people like that. Once they see you're weak, that you won't put up any resistance, they'll walk all over you your whole life."

We were in the car at that point, and the lecture continued. I listened, but I knew his diatribe would do little good. It simply wasn't in my character to fight; I was terrified by the notion. Getting hurt wasn't my biggest concern, though I'm sure some part of me feared being bloodied. But I frequently wrestled and playfully fought with my friends. Sometimes it got rough. We played sandlot football, tackling each other on the hard soil behind Mike's house with bumps, bruises, and strawberries galore. There was another psychological barrier I couldn't overcome: an utter revulsion to the idea of a physical contest with someone I didn't know, in all-out fury. I didn't have the stomach for it. I felt anxious and almost nauseated on the playground when other boys fought. While kids from every direction would stream toward the spectacle, I skulked away in the other direction, putting as much distance between myself and the altercation as possible.

When Dad and I got home, I hung my head and went to my room to think about what had happened. I began to play with my tiny soldiers, bringing one detachment after another into furious conflict with their enemies. I was sure that if I were in the army, when thrust into battle, I'd be able to hold the line and defend my country. Soldiers fought from afar with guns, mortars, and grenades, not wrestling each other or throwing punches or pulling hair. Death and injury came almost impersonally and, in my view, honorably.

As I rearranged the lines of battle, I heard my father describing the situation to my mother, his outrage apparent in the tone of his voice. My mother, ever my defender, sought to calm him and soften the severity of the whole episode.

"Jerry, he was a much older and bigger boy. Why would you expect Steve to fight him?"

"Because I can't always come riding up to save him, that's why. He's got to be able to stick up for himself—or at least put up some kind of resistance. You know, Gerry, word of this type of thing gets around, and every jerk in the neighborhood who fancies himself a bully begins to look for the weak kid and humiliate him."

This had played out many times before in our house. I made my dad happy and proud in some ways, but my behavior brought this particular issue to the forefront again and again. To my father's frustration, my reticence, introversion, self-effacement, and complete lack of assertiveness were deeply ingrained in my personality. And, to make matters worse, my sister was nearly the polar opposite of me: She was more outspoken, taller, had a bigger frame, and was neither easily subdued nor readily intimidated. When she wanted something, she went after it. The trouble was that the things she wanted often didn't coincide with what my parents thought was best for her. So they had their work cut out for them with both of their kids.

As I lay on the floor, I thought about how I was rapidly approaching middle school, which meant I'd soon run into some harsh social realities. Bigger kids. Meaner kids. And it would no longer be so easy to simply retreat to my room, indulging in my dreams while playing with miniature trains and toy soldiers. The rows of diminutive troops stood mutely in front of me as I wistfully inspected them. I'd spent many hours painting their uniforms and weapons, meticulously highlighting the tiniest details. But I knew it would soon be time to set them aside, along with the gliders, electric locomotives, and parachute men, however difficult that was likely to be. My father's frustration with my behavior had made that achingly clear.

Twenty-Four

It was with great anticipation, and some trepidation, that I threw myself into that third baseball season. I was more conscious that I was competing with other boys: If I struck out or missed the ball in the field, I would be the object of scorn. I worried about my father's expectations, the judgment of the other boys on the team, and whether or not I could develop greater skills on the diamond. This sort of gnawing anxiety touched many aspects of my life; baseball was merely the most obvious situation because my performance was so visible.

But while I struggled in athletic endeavors, I did have aspirations. If I could just overcome whatever obstacle separated me from the unflinching assertiveness I saw in the successful boys, I, too, could join the ranks of the heralded, gaining the admiration of my teammates, the coach, and even my father. I hadn't defined the problem precisely, but at least I was attaining some sense of myself. I had begun to see that something was wrong and that I was the one who had to correct it. I could not simply depend on the law of averages.

"You're gonna love this," I told Mike. "We're playing in the minor league."

He shrugged. Mike had played a lot of baseball back at his last duty station in Alabama, but he wasn't aware of some of the subtleties of our system.

I skipped ahead, then turned to face him. "Last year, and the year before, I was in the pee-wees. We played on that little field that's farthest from the school. Hardly anyone ever came to watch. The bleachers are small, and the field gets soggy if it rains. Now, we'll be on the minor league field . . . bigger bleachers, more fans, and closer to the refreshment stand!"

"That sounds great." Mike was matter of fact in his reply, but I could tell he was excited to start the season.

In the minor league, we would be issued uniforms! Actual baseball uniforms, not just T-shirts that said "Tigers" on them, that we wore shamefully with blue jeans and maroon ball caps in the pee-wees. Our Toros uniforms were light gray, with maroon piping, and had striped stirrup socks that protruded from our knicker-length trousers down to the footwear. And, instead of mere sneakers, we would wear cleats! I truly felt like a baseball player when I donned this ensemble. When no one was looking, I took to admiring myself in the mirror. I'd even do a few mock pitches from the stretch, peering intently over my shoulder at a phantom baserunner, perfecting my move to first base, and dreaming of picking off the unwary opponent.

"Batter up!" the umpire called.

It was opening day, and things were going well: we were already winning 3-to-nothing, and it would be my first at-bat of the season.

I stepped into the left-hander's box and took a practice swing. Doubtless, some of the fielders knew me and how much trouble I'd had hitting the ball the last two years. I sensed the outfielders moving in as I awaited the first pitch.

I could hear Mrs. Reimolds cheering for me in the stands, and I was encouraged. My father and mother were quieter, but I knew they were there.

"No batter, no batter, no batter," came the chatter from the infield. The phrase was the same one the fielders used for everyone, but it felt personal to me.

I froze, watching the pitcher as he performed his windup. He was a tall right-hander with an impudent grin permanently etched on his pale face.

He hurled the ball right down the middle of the plate, and I swung, meeting it a bit late but feeling the satisfying crack of the bat. I tore off toward first as the ball hopped to the waiting third baseman. He crouched and fielded the ball cleanly; I redoubled my efforts to get to first. I was looking at the first baseman as I ran, watching the expression on his face, saw his eyes widen as the ball approached, saw him bend to scoop it out of the dirt, and, just as I arrived, the ball hopped up off of the heel of his glove, careening against his chest and down into the dirt in front of him. A hit!

My mother, who was apt to keep her opinions to herself when she was in the stands, went wild. "Way to go, Steve O!" she called, clapping in unison with my father and Mrs. Reimolds.

I looked at them, bowing my head and allowing a proud smile to cross my face. I stood on the base and leaned toward second, anticipating the pitch. At the minor league level, baserunners could lead off the base during the windup and steal if the opportunity presented itself.

"Get a lead," the assistant coach said from a few feet away. "Just watch for the throw to first."

I inched down the baseline, peering intently at the pitcher, who watched me with equal intensity. I didn't want to undo what I'd been able to accomplish, and the coach had to keep urging me to move farther from the base.

My teammate took a ball, stepped back into the box, and smacked a hard grounder right back to the pitcher. I was racing toward second, and, to my surprise, the pitcher fielded the ball cleanly, turned, and threw me out. It was shocking to see efficient infield play at our level, but he looked mighty good when he scooped up that ball. I trotted back toward the dugout to a chorus of congratulations from my teammates and Mr. Gray, the coach. He patted me on the back as I arrived.

"That's the way, Steven," he announced, loud enough for the others to hear.

That set the tone for the rest of the season. I was no longer the kid who couldn't hit the ball. I did strike out sometimes, but far more commonly, I made contact. The ball seldom left the infield, but I was speedy enough, and the fielders incompetent enough, that I often outran the throws. To my utter astonishment, I was considered a real contributor to the team.

Importantly, my father took real pride in my newfound competence on the diamond. He and I would throw the ball back and forth between baseball practice days in our front yard. Part of our lawn, crowning the hill that led down to Mark's unit, was pretty flat, with our clothesline running across it. Through all the trials and tribulations of our daily existence, he and I held court during games of catch in the front yard.

He frequently announced his favorite pitchers from the golden era of baseball, many from his beloved Yankees, as he tried to mimic their deliveries.

"Tommy Davis," he noted, rearing back to deliver his fastball. Luckily, he kept it pretty tame for me.

Next, it was Sandy Koufax.

Sometimes he'd pitch out of the stretch, eyeing the imaginary baserunner before tossing the pitch to me.

"Watch out for the knuckleball," he warned as a slow, gyrating ball came my way.

I struggled to put my glove in front of it, though it hit off the heel and plopped to the ground.

I scooped it up and performed a windup that mimicked one I'd seen Dad do a hundred times.

"Here comes the heater," I warned.

As sometimes happened, the ball went a bit wild, just out of his reach. I winced. "Sorry, Dad."

I was pleased that he didn't get upset. He just turned and trotted over the hill to retrieve it. I hoped that I'd eventually attain better control.

The end of school was approaching, and we began to experience that giddy feeling that comes over schoolchildren as they contemplate the joyous freedom of summer. The baseball season was also heating up; several teams were competing for the top spot in our league. Fortunately, the Toros were one of them. But while we had started strong, we were having a late-season slump. Every game counted as we looked toward the end of the season and the standings. At that crucial time, one of our pitchers hurt his arm and another had to leave town for a week with his family. That left only two pitchers on the team. At our next practice, Mr. Gray approached me and asked if I was still interested in pitching if the opportunity should arise. Surprised by his offer, I nodded vigorously, sensing that my time had come.

I rushed home that evening.

"Dad, Dad! Mr. Gray said he'd let me pitch!"

He looked impressed. "Great, Tom. Do you know when?"

"Sometime . . . soon I hope."

I didn't have to wait long. A few days later, we played a team called the Picadors, who were pretty good and getting better as the season progressed. Our hold on first place had become tenuous. On a sunny, cloudless Friday afternoon, with the bleachers filled, we battled the Picadors to a 2-2 deadlock through the first four innings. During my second at-bat, I hit a grounder that advanced a runner who eventually scored. I also stopped a ball that dribbled out to me in the outfield, holding the runner with an accurate throw to second base. By the end of the fourth inning, our pitcher had become noticeably wild, repeatedly throwing the ball into the dirt in front of the plate. With the bases loaded, he managed to get a ground out that ended the inning.

"Steve, do you want to pitch this inning?" Mr. Gray asked me as I ran into the dugout.

I was dumbstruck. I didn't believe that I'd ever have the opportunity to pitch during a game. I saw a few heads turn; my teammates were as surprised as I was.

"Yeah—of course!" I said excitedly.

I ran to the side of the dugout and asked Pepe, our catcher, to warm me up. Neither of us was coming up to bat soon, so I measured out the distance and got my arm loose. I felt good, and I seemed to have control. I espied my father watching me from the bleachers and felt an especially intense desire to step onto the mound. After two years of obscurity in the outfield, I would finally be able to show him my abilities.

We didn't manage a hit during that inning, and the other team's fielders came off the field briskly, brimming with confidence, poised to upset the division leaders. I had been chosen to stand in their way.

I walked out to the mound, surprised at how far it suddenly seemed from the pitcher's rubber down to home plate. Pepe, a mellow and friendly boy with a caramel complexion and wiry hair, was quite large for his age. He squatted behind the plate, coaxing me. I tossed a couple of easy practice pitches, and the first Picador stepped up to the plate. He grinned at me, not with a friendly expression, but with an undisguised challenge.

"C'mon, Steve, put her in there," called Pepe. The other fielders chimed in with their chatter.

I did my windup, staring intently at his outthrust mitt.

A booming voice from the other dugout called out as my arm came forward.

"This guy stinks! This guy can't pitch!"

The ball sailed high over Pepe's head. Even though he used all his height, jumping up from his squatting position, he couldn't catch it.

I looked at the other dugout. There was a boy in there, not dressed in the uniform, probably an older kid who helped out with coaching for their team. Maybe somebody's brother. He was an imposing figure, contorting his face, laughing and pointing at me. He loudly berated me to the other boys around him, who seemed to catch the fever and all of them began a derogatory chant.

"Try it again, loser! You couldn't hit the side of a barn!"

I took the ball, wound up, and threw as hard as I could. Again, the ball sailed high, and the boys in the other dugout, led by their ringmaster, had a field day at my expense. I felt anger burning inside me. I knew I had more ability than I was showing. For the third time, I wound up, glaring at the plate, and drilled the ball toward Pepe. The ball bounced in the dirt in front of him, and the batter shook his head as if frustrated that he was facing such an inferior pitcher. The calls from the other dugout drowned out the calls of support from my own dugout and the chatter of my fielders. My fourth pitch was high and outside, though it was catchable. The batter smugly trotted off to first base while the boys on the other team went wild with excitement.

The big kid's voice was clear above all the others, unrestrained in his put-downs and name-calling. I looked down and kicked the dirt, growing more frustrated by the minute. Mr. Gray came out to talk to me.

"Steve, what's the matter? You can't let these guys get to you. I've seen you pitch at practice. You can throw strikes. You've got to focus."

I pointed at the other dugout, trying to blink away tears of frustration that had begun to well up in my eyes. "Who is he? Why is he in there?"

I could see the big guy, proud to be singled out, nodding to the boys around him, laughing at my protest.

"You have to ignore him. You have a job to do. He's with their team, he's allowed to yell at you. Now, can you pitch?"

I nodded and ground my teeth together. Looking around at my own fielders, I noticed they seemed stunned at my reaction. Their chatter had grown softer in the face of the scorn pouring out of the other dugout. The next batter, a short, chubby kid with a face dotted with freckles, stepped into the box.

I went into a stretch, looking at the runner on first. He glared back at me, daring me to throw to first, inching toward second. I wasn't buying it. I didn't think he'd steal, and I gripped the ball impossibly tight, reared back, and fired for home. The batter stepped back quickly, as the ball nearly hit him, and Pepe could not control it as it whizzed inside.

As the expected jeers rang out, I hung my head, and the runner trotted casually to second. I over-corrected, and the next pitch went outside, and then the next. The crowd behind the other team's dugout was ecstatic, and the group behind our dugout was silent. Seven straight bad pitches and none was even close to being a strike. By this time, I knew my teammates were murmuring that the coach should put another pitcher on the mound.

I looked at my hand and saw it was shaking. I was about to lose control of the situation and could not restrain my emotional reaction. Despite all my efforts, tears began to trickle down my face, and I tried to brush them away with my shirtsleeve so that no one would see. The big guy was the first to seize on my display of weakness.

"He's bawling! He's bawling!"

The crowd of boys around him were even more delighted, and there was a veritable frenzy of name-calling. I could barely see when I threw the next pitch, which had a lot on it but was wildly high. The batter tossed his bat toward the dugout, smiling at his teammates as he trotted deliberately toward first base.

I did not dare to look at my father. The tears then began to flow freely, but for some reason, Mr. Gray left me on the mound. Maybe he thought I'd get a hold of myself and break through this personal calamity, perhaps even experience some sort of shining personal enrichment. Nothing of the sort happened. Unfortunately, I was beyond any redemption at this point and yielded yet another walk to one of their batters. I was utterly distraught, yet I could not leave my post.

The next batter came up, and I managed a strike, which he swung at and fouled off. There was a smattering of applause from our bleachers, and I felt the rise of resentment within me. Fingering the ball, I glared at Pepe's mitt, went through my windup, and let fly with my hardest fastball. Far outside, the ball careened off the catcher's glove, and he turned to pursue it as hastily as he could. The lead runner, who was by this time on third, saw the passed ball and charged toward home plate while I watched, frozen with indecision.

"Home, Steve, cover home!" I heard the calls from our dugout, but I didn't process them.

Pepe grabbed the ball and turned to throw it to me, only to find that I was still standing on the mound. I was so caught up in my failings that

I had forgotten to cover home plate. The other two runners had easily moved up, and a new set of angry tears fell from my eyes.

I wiped my face, turned to the bleachers, and saw my father's stony countenance. He sat unmoving, not a trace of emotion on his face. I had disgraced him. My next three pitches were outside the strike zone, and that batter was now on base. At this point, Mr. Gray decided it was better to get me off the mound before I dug a hole from which the team could not escape. He ambled slowly toward me, motioning to the outfield for another boy to replace me. He didn't seem angry, just surprised and disappointed.

"Let's get you out to center field," he suggested, without a trace of bitterness or resentment in his voice. He was nothing if not even-handed.

I turned and walked out to center, my head down. The diamond was incredibly quiet. I don't know what I expected, but suddenly, the boys from the other dugout broke out into sarcastic cheers as if thanking me for the advantage I'd provided to their team. A set of bleachers was just outside the center field fence, filled with onlookers who watched on without a sound as I marched toward them. I think every single spectator felt both pity and revulsion at my behavior.

After two quick outs on two easy grounders to the infield, a tall and athletic kid stepped into the box. He had hit the ball hard twice before in the game, and I saw Mr. Gray signaling the outfielders to move back. We all took a few steps back and waited. As the pitcher wound up, I heard the chatter begin, rise to a crescendo, and then fall silent as the ball sailed for the catcher's mitt. I was still too busy sniffling and blinking my tears away to participate.

I heard the crack of the aluminum bat but did not see the ball leaving the infield. I suddenly heard people calling to me.

"Back up, Steve!"

"You can get it!"

By the time I saw the ball, it was too late. I backpedaled and thrust my glove upward. This could have been one of those moments when the universe accommodates a dissolute soul, had I managed to catch the ball, arresting the rally of the Picadors just as effectively as I'd stoked it. But it wasn't to be, and the ball sailed just over my upheld glove, bouncing back to the fence. I raced back to grab the ball and turned, though I could see very little through my red, tearing eyes as I whipped the ball toward second base. But the runner had already raced around second and arrived at third, standing up and looking back.

"Get it in . . . just throw it in!" I could hear Mr. Gray's voice above the din.

I hurled the ball with all my might, but my errant throw forced the second baseman well into left-center field, and when the ball bounced just in front of him and off his chest, the runner turned and ran for home. The throw home was way too late, and that three-run homer put us into a hole we could not recover from. I was beyond consolation at this point and simply stared dejectedly at the ground.

At last we got out of the inning, but our team had lost its enthusiasm. We mounted no serious scoring threats in the final at-bat. As the other team turned the final out, I sat stonily on the bench. It was a ritual for the winning team to collect on the infield and call out a rhythmic chant to show its respect for the game and the losing team.

"Two-four-six-eight, who do we appreciate? Toros!" came the call, and they threw their gloves high in the air.

I felt very little appreciation.

The teams then passed by each other in single file, shaking hands. I sat still, hoping to avoid participation in the affair. Mr. Gray approached me and told me I had to go out.

"Everybody goes out to shake, Steve. It's part of the game. You had a bad day. You'll get over it. But you've got to be a good sport. Head on out there."

I wanted to tell him no, but I knew he was right. And I knew my dad wanted me out there. I kept my head down, staring at my shoes, and walked by the other boys, lightly touching their hands.

"Cry-baby." I heard it from more than a few of those Picadors.

But I was beyond caring at that point. I just needed to get away from all of them. I knew the ride home would be terrible—the idea of facing my father filled me with anxiety and shame.

I shuffled slowly toward the stands. Mrs. Reimolds, ever faithful, was there to greet me.

"Steven, they should have kicked that big boy out of the dugout. He had no business yelling at you like that."

I thanked her, but I could not raise my head. She patted me on the back and said a polite goodbye. My father was standing next to her with his arms folded. We both turned and walked to the car.

"That was quite a show you put on out there," he said quietly.

I couldn't respond.

"But it was a great lesson for your life," he added.

I didn't know what he meant, so I merely stared out the window, waiting for him to clarify.

"People will try to tear you down, especially if you're in any kind of position of authority, or if you're successful. The pitcher is the leader of the team on the field. You're a natural target. If they get you flustered, your team suffers. That's exactly what they did. Life will put you in prominent positions over and over. And then people will come at you. So you better get used to it. And you better learn to cope with it somehow. Do you understand?"

I started to cry again. I had never felt quite that wretched in my young life and nodded solemnly, hoping that would suffice.

By this time, we were in our driveway. To my chagrin, Mike stood on the carport, waving as we drove up.

"Did you guys win?"

I just shook my head and marched up the stairs. My father gave Mike the short version without dwelling too much on my reaction to the disaster. My friends would hear about it soon enough. Doubtless, I'd be branded "that kid from the Toros who cried on the mound."

I went to my room and tore off my uniform, throwing it into a heap in the corner. I sat on my bed, scowling at the pile of crumpled clothes, wishing I'd never gone out for baseball. When I looked out the window, I was startled to see that it was still a bright, sunny afternoon, that kids were out on their bikes and that there were others playing tag nearby, filling the air with their laughter. The world had failed to recognize my catastrophic event, continued turning, and paid no heed to my plight.

Soon my mother would come in, I thought, to offer her kindness and consolation. But I didn't feel I deserved such a thing, so I crept through the hall and quietly slipped out the front door. As I did, I heard my father in the kitchen, recounting every detail of the episode to my mom, who thankfully had not come to the game. The tone of his voice suggested he could barely get his mouth open to speak.

"Jerry," she protested, "it's just a baseball game!"

I wished I could have looked at the world through her rose-colored glasses at that moment.

Twenty-Five

In my childish mind, I was sure that the weight of the entire world was crashing down upon me. I ran down our steps and the hill out front, crunching across Mark's driveway then dropping down into the gullies, hoping no one would see me. There, I spent the next couple of hours wandering aimlessly, finally stopping to sit and peer up at the cloudless sky. I thought some wisdom might come to me, some celestial explanation of how this could have happened in my life, which had seemed so promising just a few hours before. Unfortunately, no such thing occurred, and I hung my head, letting the afternoon pass me by while I sat in my lonely perch.

As evening approached, I felt a pang of hunger and walked slowly back to the house. Inside, I sat at a silent table with my family and managed but a few bites of food, then went quietly to my room. My dreams that night were filled with images of my emotional breakdown. Again and again, I saw myself losing control on the field in anger and frustration as tears dribbled down my cheeks. In the dreams, much as in my life, I could not check the feelings that had welled up inside of me.

When gray dawn crept through the window, I dressed and stole outside as silently as I could, again headed for the solitude of the gullies. I found my resting spot from the day before and settled back to watch the sun rise, its warm beams slowly descending into the ravine. I leaned back against the sandy embankment, running my hands through the tiny rivulets that creased it, sending small pebbles tumbling to the bottom with a bit of a rattle. When they stopped, I was surprised to hear another sound, barely audible, just behind me.

I looked back curiously, wondering who or what might be behind me. I was startled by what I saw: Not three feet from me, resting along the embankment, was a perfect specimen of a six-lined racerunner. Perhaps the one we'd encountered a few weeks before. Though I was interested, I was emotionally exhausted from the episode the day before. I could not muster even a trace of excitement. I looked at him, as still as I could be, as he surveyed the surroundings, perhaps unaware that I was there. In my awkward position, and with none of my hunting team there to enlist for assistance, I settled on simply observing this elusive lizard. I knew I couldn't capture him. If I moved, he'd tear off with startling speed.

I began to wonder why I felt the need to imprison this delightful creature. For the moment, I had him in my possession. He wasn't going anywhere, at least not for a few precious seconds. He was perched proudly in a place where I could carefully watch him at eye level. And he was in a vast terrarium—admittedly without any glass or other barriers around him. Too often, in my own terrariums, the lizards crawled under the rocks or sticks that I placed within, and I couldn't even see them when I looked inside. But this fantastic little reptile was mine to enjoy for the next few minutes. And instead of being sluggish and sick, he was at the top of his game, tongue flickering in and out, eyes carefully scanning the ravine below him for signs of prey, tail twitching in expectation of the need to run. It was inspiring to behold him, and I certainly did "own" him for this brief time. Somehow, it was even better because I had no intention of trying to capture him. He was in his element, and I was an ideally situated observer, with nothing artificial between myself and this fabled specimen.

"There he is!"

I heard Mark's familiar voice as he came rushing through the sagebrush. In an instant, the startled lizard scampered over the brim of the gully and rushed headlong down the slope next to me. Reflexively, I reached down—and he was in my grasp! He froze, lying in my trembling hand in a most docile way. Even his fine, whiplike tail had ceased to move. If lizards said prayers, I assumed he was busy saying them then.

"You got him!" Mark cried, coming up to the edge of the ditch. Mike was right behind him, startled and excited.

In that thrilling moment, I had forgotten my woes. "*We* got him. You chased him right to me!" I cried. I held him up for the others to see.

Mark shook his head, amazed. Then he looked at me. "What's wrong with you? And why were you down here by yourself?" My eyes must have been pretty red.

I hung my head, not really in a frame of mind to report what had happened. "Yesterday was a really bad day."

Mike looked at me knowingly. Thankfully, he declined to offer any details, and I couldn't elaborate. The shame burned too intensely, and I simply had to turn away from what I had done.

"Let's get him up to the bucket on your porch."

"Yeah," Mark exclaimed. "We'll build the best terrarium ever. We can take him around to show the other guys."

We marched triumphantly up to my porch, ascending the stairs like conquering heroes.

"We got him," Mark cried. "We finally got him!"

I held the six-lined racerunner close to me, firmly, but not too forcefully, lest I should injure him. I could feel his small chest expanding as he breathed. I had never counted a lizard's breathing rate, but he seemed to be breathing awfully fast.

"He's probably scared to death," I muttered.

Mike and Mark had returned the bucket to the gully to gather authentic artifacts from his environment. We thought that they would be better for his sense of security. Soon the two returned, the bottom of the pail congested with sticks, stones, and little mounds of sandy soil.

We put the pail on a rickety picnic table that sat on the terraza, and I lowered him in. He lay perfectly still, breathing rapidly.

"He's beautiful," Mike said, drawing a breath.

"Yeah," I agreed.

But it didn't feel right. I'd seen this proud lizard in his element, vigilant, wary, and perched on the edge of danger. Now, he was in a bucket with some rocks, to be fed lousy food that he probably wouldn't even eat. His perspective would be limited to gazing a few inches in any direction, the opalescent plastic of the container barely allowing the sun's glow to filter through.

I thought hard about what had come to pass for this handsome creature and about my own comeuppance the day before. The opportunity to pitch meant everything to me, and I had allowed my own ego to ruin my one and only outing.

"We can't keep him," I suddenly announced.

"What?" They raised their voices in unison.

"We got him. We know it. He's the best lizard out there by far. We've got to put him back. Look at him. He won't move. He's terrified. He might even be in shock. Putting them in this bucket does something bad to these lizards—we can't let that happen to him."

There was a stunned silence. Then a murmur of recognition. Mark was particularly stricken but willing to see my point of view. He frowned. "Yeah. I guess so. But who's gonna believe that we ever caught him?"

The other boys in Royal Oaks needed to see and understand our accomplishment. I thought about that for a few seconds. "My sister got one of those cameras for Christmas that takes an instant picture. We could get a picture of him to show to everyone!"

I ran inside to get Kathy's Polaroid "Swinger" and returned to find them both peering lovingly over the edge of the bucket. We had done something special. I snapped a photo of our captive, who lay provocatively on a bed of light-colored soil with his tail curled around him. At least he hadn't run under one of the sticks.

"Cool." Mark's pride was evident.

"Well, this way, we've always got him," Mike added.

I reached in and carefully lifted him out. Everyone took a turn holding him, and then I gently folded my hands around him for the brief trip back to the gully. We walked back down the stairs and descended into the labyrinth of sandy arroyos to the lizard's home, much more subdued than we had been on the way up.

I found my way back to the very same trench, and my friends stood along the brim as I placed him where I had first seen him. He paused momentarily, sampling his freedom with an inquisitive tongue, and then scurried rapidly in the other direction.

Our small assembly remained silent, and then we turned for home.

"That was really cool." Mike was beaming.

That evening, I sat beside my father at the dinner table. It was just him and me, as my sister had already eaten and run out to some activity or other. Mom was still in the kitchen, getting things together.

I looked at him and held my head up, something I'd been unable to do the day before. His manner had softened somewhat. I guessed that he'd come to terms with my actions and realized that neither his world nor mine had come to an end. At least, by that point, I had.

"Guess what, Dad?"

He gave me the look. I knew what his answer would be, so I quickly spoke up.

"We caught him today. After three years of trying."

"Caught who?"

"The six-lined racerunner. You know, the fastest lizard anywhere. We saw him a few weeks ago—I told you, remember?"

Dad nodded, appearing to have some memory of the incident. "How'd you catch him?"

"Teamwork," I said deliberately. I needed my father to know that I understood the concept and had badly misapplied it in my debacle on the pitching mound.

He took my meaning, carefully suppressing a smile with his thin lips. "Well, where did you guys put him?" he asked, assuming we had him in captivity somewhere.

"We took him up on the terraza for a while, you know, so we could check him out, but then we put him back. I think he belongs out there, in the gullies. I took a picture of him—see?"

Dad was suitably impressed. "That's a fast-looking lizard, all right. Racing stripes and all. But I'm glad you put him back."

I nodded, allowing myself to recover just a bit of my pride. "Me too, Dad. Me too."

Twenty-Six

"Steve, you have to go over to Mr. Gray's house and give him the uniform yourself."

I swallowed hard.

With only three games left in our season, I had told the coach of the Toros that I would be missing a game in order to go to the local amusement park in Madrid, an annual outing to celebrate my birthday.

"Really, Steve, we need you—I don't think we'll have enough players," Mr. Gray had explained.

"But it's my birthday. My dad took the day off and everything!"

My coach had been steadfast in his insistence that I come to the game. If I didn't show up on Friday, he told me, I would be off the team. That was a difficult situation for me—my father *hated* quitting. In my mind, however, I was being kicked off the team. I didn't really want to stop playing baseball; I just didn't want to stand on the pitcher's mound again.

"Steve, are you sure it's worth it? I can probably get another day off," my father offered when he learned of the conflict.

But I would not be dissuaded. "We've been planning this for months. Mike is coming with us. We bought the same shorts to wear and everything!"

It was almost true. Our mothers had coincidentally picked up the same white, fringed shorts with red and blue checks on them at the base exchange. When we discovered we had the same pair, we were elated, and resolved to wear them to the amusement park together.

Even though he was unhappy about me leaving the team, I think my father could see that I was standing up for something I really wanted, and, as he would have phrased it, "showing some backbone." Still, Dad wanted to make certain that I would take full responsibility for my decision. I was more than a little put out by his demand. I envisioned myself standing meekly at Mr. Gray's door, while he scowled at me as I told him I'd made up my mind to go to the amusement park instead of the game.

"Well, *I'm* not going to take it to him. You have to be the one to do it, Steve."

I set my jaw and accepted the challenge. "OK. I will."

I'm pretty sure Dad thought I'd chicken out and give up on the birthday trip.

Walking briskly back to my room, I took my Toros uniform out of the drawer, along with the cool stirrup socks. I looked fondly at the maroon hat and thought I would keep that. Folding the clothes into a neat pile, I walked over to the Grays' quarters, just one unit over. I trotted up the stairs and was satisfied as I came up onto their terraza that all was quiet. Tiptoeing to the front door, I hoped with all my might that Mr. Gray and his family weren't home. I then placed the uniform carefully on the welcome mat, rang the bell, and hastily made my way back toward the steps. Unfortunately, the door opened within a matter of seconds, and I heard the coach call my name.

"Steve, wait, now. Are you sure you want to do this?"

I looked at him and nodded, swallowing hard.

"We really need you that day. Can't the amusement park wait?"

"It's my birthday," I emphasized.

I couldn't bear the thought of changing the date of our perfectly planned outing. And somehow, despite my intentions, Mr. Gray was making me quit the team instead of simply letting me go. I didn't understand how the tables got turned—I should have asked him if *he* was sure that *he* wanted to do this, but that thought did not occur to me at the moment.

"All right, then," he said, his deep voice surprisingly gentle. He picked up the uniform and went back inside.

I felt strangely sad and free at the same time as I walked back to my home, my hands in my pockets.

Three days later, we went to the amusement park, as scheduled, without another word regarding the Toros. I really had no major regrets, though I was a bit wistful when I learned that the team outlasted the various challengers and narrowly maintained their position in first place in our league. Perhaps it should not have been a surprise that I did not receive an invitation to the team picnic, news I greeted with a tinge of bitterness. I'd been there for eighteen of the twenty-one games. But, as my father noted, it was probably appropriate given the choice I'd made. And after my awful behavior on that one gruesome, unforgettable afternoon, I was somewhat embarrassed by the idea of going to a party with the rest of my team members, anyway.

But the day at Casa de Campo was sublime.

Amusement parks by their very nature encouraged independence, exploration, and intricate planning. My mom set us free, telling us where and when to meet up with my parents, to periodically check-in. I found great satisfaction in looking at the little map with which we were provided, figuring out which rides were where, and developing our strategy. But this meticulous plotting, as I joyfully anticipated our movement around the park, was tedious for Mike. He wanted to get where we were going, jump on the ride, and then decide where to go next.

"Why do we have to figure out every ride we're going to go to now?" Mike asked, just after I'd secured the map at the entrance kiosk.

"Well, look at this layout of the park," I countered, pointing to the colorful fold-up pamphlet that neither of us could quite understand.

Despite the language barrier, the pictures were quite helpful; at least you could tell a Ferris wheel from a roller coaster.

"Here's the Volcano. We're gonna love that. We'll start there. After we get through that, we'll make our way over to the German swings, and that Scrambler thing. And I can do the teacups and the whip. They're right along this inner corridor," I explained.

I must have sounded like Napoleon, optimistically scheduling his conquest of one town after the next as he swept through Europe.

Mike groaned. I was over-organizing an adventure that was supposed to be fun and unstructured. Clearly, spontaneity was not my strong point. But I did derive great enjoyment from planning and carefully pursuing the projected activities. For someone as carefree and effervescent as Mike, that was pretty restrictive. But we both liked to eat, and we had some money. So I made a point of interspersing some stops between the rides and other activities for amusement park treats.

"Right here, between the swings and the Scrambler, we can get some French fries," I explained, trying to soothe his offended sensibilities.

"You mean the Octopus?" he asked, looking interested.

"No. Not the Octopus—it's called the Scrambler. It's like the Octopus, but it doesn't go up in the air. I can't go on the Octopus. I'll throw up."

Mike looked dubious. He may not have ridden that particular ride before, or maybe they didn't call it a Scrambler at the other parks he'd been to. He didn't seem to think it would be that much fun. At any rate, I was able to convince him that there was a lot to be happy about.

"Look, this volcano thing is gonna be a blast. It's like a gigantic model that's supposed to have fire, lava, and smoke." I was doing my best to interpret the description on the map.

"It sounds kind of boring." Mike was unconvinced.

Casa de Campo was a joyful place, and no tickets were required. Once you paid, you were free to get on any ride if you could stand in line long enough. Fortunately, the rides I chose seldom had much of a line, so we were able to do a lot instead of waiting in long lines for exciting rides.

The Volcano was more of an experience than a ride, but it was fascinating to me. After entering a well-simulated cavern, which smelled of brimstone, we were led onto an elevator with the few fun-lovers besides ourselves who had chosen to come in. The doors shut and we began our descent, heading miles below the surface. Well, that's what we were told, anyway, as best we could understand. The doors opened to a fantastic sight.

"Wow," Mike said, ogling the coarse rock walls.

Massive gemstones protruded from the sides and floor of the tunnel, and these had been cleverly illuminated to fill the passages through which we walked with multicolored hues. I found it awe-inspiring, a scene right out of *Star Trek*.

We made our way through a series of these corridors, enchanted by our surroundings, until we came to a dark passage that led to a coarse, rocky staircase that took us up to another level. Here, the passages were filled with a strange vapor that made our journey even more mysterious. Wisps of smoke curled through the succession of chambers we found ourselves in, and a profound, almost tangible rumbling echoed through the tunnels, growing louder as we moved along. Another staircase hewn into the simulated rock presented itself, at the top of which there was a fiery red glow illuminating the walls of the cave. There was a simmering sound, along with the loud rumbling, and the smell of something burning was much stronger.

On this level we encountered two Spanish girls who were chattering to each other and laughing. They held hands as they moved before us on the path, as young girls in Europe often do. One of them had long, wavy hair and large brown eyes that startled me when my own eyes met them. After looking back at us, she giggled with her friend, and the two moved rapidly ahead, as though afraid they might have to speak with us if we remained so close. I watched them disappear ahead into the smoke and turned to Mike. He gave me one of his "why not" smiles, dimples and all, and we sped forward to maintain some proximity to them. Turning a corner, we were nearly blinded by the smoke.

"I don't see them, do you?" Mike bent low, squinting through the mist. The girls were nowhere to be seen.

"Figures," I thought. In truth, I knew I wasn't likely to strike up a conversation with a young Spanish girl, no matter how captivating her charms, but I now had grounds to sulk about it.

We moved cautiously up the rugged steps and found ourselves in another large chamber at the center of which was a pool of molten lava flowing in a stream along the floor of the cave. A narrow trail led around this simulated lava pool, which was evidently heated, because it was very hot in there. A small rock bridge led over the stream to the doors of a waiting elevator. I hoped the girls would be on it as well, but we were by ourselves.

"That was neat." Mike giggled as we got off, and I agreed wholeheartedly.

"See, I told you!" This was a moment of great satisfaction for me.

We both felt like we'd been to the center of the earth. I was kind of proud of myself for steering us to this exciting experience. Really, it was right up my alley: active, educational, exciting, and without fast motions that made me feel out of control.

"You were right," he admitted and, without missing a beat, went on to his own plan. "Let's go have some real fun!"

I couldn't keep us off the rides forever, and off we went to spin and laugh and eat. I was careful to guide us to the kinder, gentler ones that I could handle.

My father never ceased trying to get me to step beyond my fears. It irritated him that I wouldn't ride the more exhilarating amusements. He happened to see us by the Octopus, after we'd been on the series of kiddie rides I'd selected.

"C'mon, Steve," he said, his hands resting impatiently on his hips. "I'll ride with you and Mike. Once you get on this thing, you'll have a blast. You just have to get on it."

I stood my ground and shook my head sullenly. A few Spanish kids stepped tenderly past us, perhaps sensing the tension between my father and me. They took their places on the ride and chattered happily. One of them said derisively, "Este nino tiene miedo," as a commentary on my apparent fear. I may have been overly sensitive on the point, and they did talk awfully fast, but I was pretty sure that's what I heard him say.

I had once come unglued on a version of that Octopus ride, in a small amusement park in the West View neighborhood of Pittsburgh, screaming over and over until the operator stopped it, allowing me to get off to the relief and satisfaction of everyone else on the ride. Although I'd been a lot younger then, I needed to make sure I wouldn't go through that again or put the other riders through it.

"All right, Steve. I give up. You can stand here and watch us. C'mon, Mike."

The two of them got into one of the little tentacle cars, and off they went. I watched them spin and rise and fall and spin some more, laughing and holding on to the safety bar. It was fun to see my father so animated, in a way he seldom appeared, and I felt a tinge of regret that I wasn't able to make him feel that way with my own companionship. He was up there with my friend, and I couldn't muster the courage to get on the Octopus, or "El Pulpo," as the ride was called in Spanish. I could not seem to find the enjoyment others found in falling, rising, or spinning at high velocity. Instead, the feelings filled me with terror, a sense of losing control, and nausea. I just didn't get it. I'm sure in my father's eyes it was consistent with the relative meekness I displayed in so many facets of life.

Mike staggered off El Pulpo, and I guided him to a bench where we laughed about his experience with my dad. A few French fries later, we headed off to explore another section of the Casa de Campo, and then head back to the Volcano for one last run through the center of the earth before we had to pack it up.

"I can't believe it's over." I was wistful, looking back over my shoulder at the rides, which were now illuminated and beckoned us to return.

"Me neither. Everything fun always goes so fast." Mike had a knack for saying just the right thing to capture the moment.

With darkness falling over us, we walked back through the enormous fairgrounds where the prize-winning livestock were kept. Casa de Campo was a sort of a fair and amusement park all in one, and a tremendous draw for people from all over Spain. In the fourth grade, our class had taken a field trip there, and we spent the day with the various animals and farm exhibitions. One of the pens had held a ferocious black bull that would someday make its way to the bullring. On that day, it merely stood still and ate some type of grain, calmly surveying the crowd, which was busy ogling him.

"Sounds like Ferdinand," Mike mused.

"Yeah, he was just like Ferdinand. I don't think he made a very good bullfight!"

We both laughed at this as we arrived at our car. On the way home, I pored over our map as best I could in the failing light, tracing and re-tracing our route through the park, marking our adventures in my mind at every ride and food stand we had gone to. Mike feigned interest, but he was pretty tired, and the darkness, warmth, and exhaustion soon overcame him. As he drifted off to sleep, I sat staring happily out the window once it became too dark to follow our steps on the paper plan of Casa de Campo.

Twenty-Seven

"One more day!" Mark could hardly contain himself. I thought he might break out into a little jig right there at the bus stop.

No one else paid much attention, but everyone understood.

So many good things were happening just then, for Mark and for me. I knew he was filled with joy, not only because school was about to end but because he'd be heading back to the States in just a few weeks.

We waved goodbye as he walked up those steps onto the wheezing school bus for the last time during his time in Spain, and Mike and I turned to walk down into the gullies. The final day of school was upon us. We'd spent the last few days immersed in activities devised to keep us busy but which were barely constructive. Most of us found it impossible to control our excitement. The learning was over, and we were on the threshold of freedom and unbridled joy. At recess, we were louder and more contentious; the dodgeball was thrown with greater energy; every game we indulged in was somehow more keen-edged and fun.

And presiding over us with his gentle demeanor and almost limitless patience was Mr. Walden. He relished his hours with us even more as our time grew short. On that day of great expectation, one day before the final day, he herded us onto the stage in the auditorium for our long-awaited assembly.

"OK, OK. Line up, everyone." He quickly and carefully arranged us in the order he preferred as we paraded onto the stage. "Mauro, where's your hat?"

My friend looked bewildered. Clearly, he'd forgotten it.

"Never mind, here's an extra." Never angry, our teacher was always prepared. Mauro nodded in relief.

With exuberance and pride, we displayed our talent and dedication as we performed a series of dances, each representing a different country: the Mexican hat dance, the Irish jig, a Spanish dance with a name I cannot remember. And Kelly, my secret heartthrob, had a ballet solo. I almost melted as I watched her performing under the lights, as graceful as any dancer I'd ever seen. We had practiced those dances for months, and Mr. Walden beamed as we bowed to the applause of the third- and fourth-graders who'd come to see our show.

The next day, our last day of school in the fifth grade, he walked among us in the classroom, his arms filled with hardback books bound in red cloth.

"This is it—the book you've each created."

He had a particular expression of satisfaction as he regarded us. Each book displayed on its cover four simple words: "My Fifth-Grade Work." Many of us had forgotten, in our excitement, that a month before, he'd collected a large sample of our reports, papers, and artwork from each of us.

Approaching us individually at our desks, Mr. Walden proudly presented the books. The murmuring grew as he handed each one to its excited owner, who quickly flipped through it to reveal a summary of our many activities for the year.

"Aren't they beautiful?" he asked, aware of our reactions. "With all the hard work you've done this year, I wanted to leave you with something you could always remember me by, something that captured the spirit of our time together and all your hard work."

I was thrilled as I looked through my own version. We'd accomplished so much over the course of the school year. Vivid memories flowed through my mind as I paged my way through. It wasn't hard to see that many of my efforts, whether in penmanship, book reports, or test results, had improved as the year progressed. It was a visible reminder of the development he'd fostered within me, within all of us.

Abruptly, the final bell sounded, and our year with Mr. Walden ended. Like my classmates, I was dazed by the euphoria that children feel when they are liberated from school for another summer. Still, I began to feel a bittersweet sensation inside. A sadness befell me as Mr. Walden quietly observed our energetic preparations to rush to the door.

I realized I was leaving behind the finest teacher I'd ever had. I, like Mark, would be leaving soon to go back home. I knew that I would enter a new school with new acquaintances in an urban neighborhood that was barely familiar while awaiting my father to take me to a strange town and yet another school only a few months after that. Even though I was excited to return to the United States, with all its excitement, familiarity, and promise, I would also be leaving behind my best friends, my favorite past-times, our lizard-catching adventures, and the familiar paths and topography that had marked my life for years. I looked up expectantly.

"This is quite simply one of the finest classes I've ever had," my teacher announced, looking around the room with what I thought was a glint in his eye. "I will miss you all quite a lot."

He took out a hanky, wiped his nose gingerly, then replaced it inside the breast pocket of his jacket. And with that, we were dismissed.

I became aware of a soft sound released from dozens of anxious throats, which slowly grew into a roar of elation. There was a veritable stampede for the door, and twenty-five anxious students rushed into a frenzied bottleneck. The halls outside boomed with revelry as teachers channeled their classes to the doors.

I stopped at the entryway and turned around. Mr. Walden was watching us, leaning on his desk as he often did when reading to the class.

"Mr. Walden?" I said softly.

"Steven?"

"I just wanted to say thanks."

He looked down at his polished, wing-tip shoes, then gave me a hint of a smile. I turned to join the tumultuous parade in the hallway.

Twenty-Eight

"I didn't know if you'd come over to see me before I left." Mark was at his door, a look of relief on his freckled face.

He and his family had been busy preparing to head back to the U.S., and I hadn't seen much of him, so I walked down to his quarters about a week after school ended. The movers had come and gone, and his house was almost empty. On my way up his stairs, I noticed the crypt we'd constructed for the unfortunate lizard the previous autumn, wondering what would become of it after we left. Doubtless, the carcass had withered and broken down by this point into an unrecognizable fibrous mass that, if it fell into the dirt, would be almost impossible to distinguish from the matter around it. I felt a little withered inside myself as I stood before my friend, not quite ready to believe that this might be the last time we'd see each other.

"Course I would," I replied to him as sincerely as I could. I appreciated the gentle smile that reflected his ready acceptance of the episodes of life as they came to him, and I knew I'd miss his winsome expression.

It was an awkward moment. I guess we didn't know quite what to say to each other.

"I'm sure glad we caught him," he suddenly said brightly, in recognition of our most celebrated accomplishment.

That short statement encompassed three years of trials, tribulations, and fond memories, a proper distillation of our friendship.

"Me too." I reached out and shook his hand. It was the manly thing to do. "See ya. I hope they have lizards wherever you guys end up."

Mark had talked about New Hampshire and Montana since I'd known him. We all had our fantasies about where we would go when the orders came to head back to the States. His family was going to Montana for a few weeks to visit his relatives, and then they would head to his dad's new duty station.

I had arrived just in time—they were soon leaving for dinner, and they would then head to the airport. Mark got into the car with his mom and dad and his gaggle of sisters, and, as I watched wistfully, they drove off, a little dust plume following the car up the driveway. I followed them up the grade, waving. As they turned onto the road, I saw Mark looking back at me. His gaze reflected, I fancied, a recognition of our good times, of movies and board games and parachute men, of the pool and the gullies, catching lizards and playing army.

I shuffled across the driveway to my house, hoping someone could give me a bit of cheer. The unstable, triangular friendship that Mark, Mike, and I had enjoyed for nearly a year was officially over. In recent months, I'd been friendlier with Mike. However, I still had fun when I spent time with Mark and was especially pleased when all three of us got along well, whether over a board game or out in the gullies.

"Mark just left—they're flying back to the States tonight," I reported as we picked up the ping-pong paddles.

Mike bobbed his head sympathetically. But he didn't seem so disappointed at Mark's departure, which I suppose was understandable. I had brought them together despite some pretty distinct personality traits and interests. I'd been a sort of bridge for our threesome. The two of them had never attended the same school, whereas Mark and I had been together at the elementary in Royal Oaks for almost three years, walking home together on the sunny Spanish afternoons. On the way, we would play chasies with our best marbles, act out scenes from our favorite movies, and talk about all the things we'd do when we got home. He had prepared me for the upcoming classes as I moved through the grades, sharing his stories of lessons, teachers, and assemblies.

After a lackluster game of ping-pong, in which Mike nearly skunked me, I made my way sullenly back up to my house. Climbing the cement steps, I stood on our terraza and looked down over the hill at Mark's quarters. It looked blank and empty. But I knew a new family would soon move in, probably within a few days, bringing their furnishings, relationships, and personalities to fill the void. The units never stayed empty for long.

All of this moving about posed a challenge. Back in the States, military people often moved in and out of neighborhoods populated by families that were timeless inhabitants of their towns, and these people, stationary and content in their surroundings, literally created the local history. But we Air Force, Army, and Navy families, on the other hand, were transients who came and went too quickly to have any true effect on the evolving culture of a place. We tumbled along like pebbles in a brook. At the same time, those who occupied these communities, the rooted people, made up the bedrock of the watercourse: life streamed by them, taking us with it, while they defined and anchored their towns and cities. Royal Oaks, like most military housing, was perceptibly different, a village of transients, a place without the history that people infuse into a region simply by existing, reproducing, and staying there. We came to expect the constant tumult of families coming and going, though we never became completely comfortable with it.

"Stevie, you've gotta come to Kids Day at the club." Mr. Mazza regarded me fondly. I could tell that he was offering something special.

I was immediately unsettled and a little reluctant to agree. "I don't know if I can get a ride. I think my dad has duty this weekend." I wasn't really so sure of that, but I thought I'd heard him allude to a weekend assignment in the near future.

"Nonsense. You'll ride with Mike and me. I'll take you in and drive you home. It'll be a blast. All the kids from the base come—food, games, prizes, swimming. It's a great party!"

My friend stood beside him, nodding enthusiastically. He was looking forward to this occasion.

Mike's special status as the son of the man who ran the Officers' Club translated into some unusual opportunities for him. He attended parties and picnics there that I would never have dreamed of going to. I sensed my place as the son of an enlisted man, though I sometimes felt a tinge of jealousy when he would come back from an outing and tell me how cool it was. Maybe it was his boldness that I envied more than his opportunities. He had no hesitancy to step into any situation and announce himself—not as someone special or exalted, but just as somebody. Someone who deserved to be there and who warranted consideration. I knew it was the right way to act in a group of strangers or at a party, at least until the ice was broken. But I shuddered at the prospect. It wasn't a comfortable approach for me.

"It's gonna be so fun. We'll have a barbecue, cake, candy. We get to swim in the pool, and they have a greasy pig contest!"

I really had no way out after Mr. Mazza offered to drive me to the picnic.

"Course . . . it sounds great!" I tried to sound enthused.

But after taking him up on it, I soon began to worry.

"Steve, you'll have a good time. Trust me," my father reassured me when I told him how I felt.

"Dad, I'm not an officer's son. They're gonna know that. I've never even been there before. Everyone will see I'm not one of them."

"It's Kids Day. Nobody is looking at you like that. You'll be with Mike and Mr. Mazza. Not one person is going to be concerned about *why* you're there. Everyone will be caught up in the fun. Honestly, people don't sit there and try to decide who's worthy of attending. It's a party—if you're there, you belong."

He made it sound so simple, but my doubts persisted. In private, Dad must have been shaking his head, wondering how his son could take an opportunity for fun and adventure and turn it into a source of inadequacy and self-doubt. He probably felt like he was raising Charlie Brown sometimes.

I had a stomachache that next morning, probably from worrying. But I reported for duty, and off we rode to the Air Force base.

"Wow, this place is really neat." I couldn't help but express my enthusiasm as we rolled up and parked.

Mr. Mazza beamed. This was his territory. The Officers' Club was a much grander affair than the NCO club, where my parents sometimes took us for hamburgers. Inside the O club, as they called it, there was a fancy dining room instead of a darkened bar with a bunch of tables arranged in front of it. Outside was a big lawn with picnic tables, white tablecloths, and pavilions—it looked like a city park. Big black grills were fired up, with hamburgers and hot dogs flying off the coals onto plates piled high. A towering cake took center stage on a table by the grills, and there were colorful streamers and balloons. It was all very festive. Kids stood around in small groups, eyeing the setting happily.

Mike went over to some friends, with me in tow, and started chatting with them. He introduced me, and I nodded. They were polite enough but not awfully interested in me, or so I perceived. After murmuring a quiet hello, I kept my peace. Soon, I drifted out of the circle and just walked around, looking things over. I ran into Mr. Mazza, who was running back and forth, ensuring things got done. He was frenetic, but he always appeared to have things under control.

"Are you having a good time, Stevie?" he asked, putting a hand on my shoulder.

I assured him I was.

"Well, get a burger. It's almost time for the greasy pig contest."

I had two juicy hamburgers. They were fantastic, and after I wolfed down some cake from a table full of treats, I joined the restless group of kids out in the middle of the yard.

The greasy pig contest was a bit anticlimactic. While most of us simply shifted around in response to the turbulent motion of the crowd, a big, aggressive kid ran the little pig down, trapping the writhing animal while it squealed in terror. I don't even know what he won. I was just happy to finally eat another piece of that phenomenal cake and avoid being conspicuous.

"Let's go swimming!"

Mike felt at home at the club, and I felt lucky to be with him.

We changed into our suits and soon splashed around in a pool almost as large as the one at Royal Oaks. I gradually began to feel more at ease. No one had challenged me, and no one had questioned my presence.

"You probably could've caught that pig. He ran right at you," Mike said, laughing and blowing water out of his nose.

"Yeah, I bet I could've," I agreed. But I had strategically stepped aside when the piglet charged toward me with a frantic crowd on its heels. The whole thing seemed kind of cruel to me.

Mike dunked me a few times, and I returned the favor. Then we practiced half-somersaults off the side, something he called a "watermelon."

After a few more snacks, it was time to go. My self-doubt and lingering anxieties had gradually slipped away. I had ventured into "Officer Country" and had a good time. And I had Mike and his father to thank for it.

Upon hearing about the festivities, my dad quickly reminded me that he'd been right.

"I know, Dad. I just have a hard time with strangers."

"Yes, you do. But it's getting better. You're growing up." He nodded with satisfaction, which gave me a pretty warm feeling inside.

Just a few weeks later, after nearly four years of anticipation, it was my family's turn to head back home to the States. I was thrilled, anxious, and reticent, in sequence, as we made our preparations to leave Torrejon and as we talked about the exciting possibilities.

"I can't wait to go back to St. Basil's. I told everyone there I'd be back!" Kathy announced at the dinner table. "Wait till I tell them all about living in Spain."

She relished the prospect that she would instantly become the center of attention. My sister was popular and always with the "in crowd," wherever we went. For that, I envied her. My mother noticed that I wasn't as thrilled about returning to Pittsburgh.

"What about you, bud? You can catch up with some of your old friends, too. Remember Ronnie?"

"Uh, yeah, Ronnie . . . Klefshankle. We had a lot of fun on the playground. What if he's not there anymore? What if he moved?"

"It's Pittsburgh, Steve. People don't move. They stay there for their entire lives." My dad smiled and shook his head as though that fact should have been obvious to me.

"And what about Isaly's? Right across the street? We can go get a skyscraper cone! Then go down to watch a movie at the theater in Mt. Oliver!" Mom was recollecting a lot of pleasant memories to put me in the right frame of mind for the move.

Kathy chimed in, ever the dispeller of euphoria, "Aunt Babe said they sold that Isaly's. Now it's called Sweet Williams. And they don't have skyscraper cones anymore."

I looked at my parents, arching my eyebrows.

"Well, I'm sure they still have chocolate ice cream and milkshakes. I'll take you and Ricky over there the first day when we get back."

She really tried to ensure that things would work out in the best possible way for her kids, no matter how hard we attempted to erect barriers in her path.

"That sounds fun," I said half-heartedly.

After dinner, in a reflective mood, I took a stroll out in front of our quarters and looked down the hill at the gullies, toward the school and ball fields that lay beyond. For almost half my life, my existence had revolved around that relatively small stretch of real estate. Between the baseball diamond, the classrooms, and the dry washes where the lizards ran, I'd experienced a great deal. There were failures I needed to acknowledge, even as I remembered the fun and camaraderie I'd enjoyed there. In the restless competition I endured with my peers, I would never be branded aggressive—this had become painfully apparent to me. I was not going to be a leader. And that would always be a sore point with my dad. But my time in Royal Oaks had taught me much: the value of loyalty, friendship, teamwork, persistence, even forgiveness.

It was time to leave Spain now, to go back to my own familiar country and start life anew. I tightened my jaw muscles and felt a tear in my eye, which I blinked away quickly. But in that moment, in the shimmering spectacle before me, I briefly saw the boy who became lost and distraught as he walked an unfamiliar road toward a new home, the boy who readily subjugated himself to another as he carried a bagful of milk cartons, the boy who wept in frustration and self-spite on the baseball diamond. I knew with certainty that I didn't want to be that boy anymore. *He* would have to remain there, on the patch of dry, furrowed, wild earth.

I would go home with a new identity, as someone who'd grown up a bit and who was now developing a sense of direction in life. And I was pretty sure I could leave a lot of childish uncertainties and fears behind me.

Afterword

Memoirs are simply a slice of life: temporally, emotionally, even geographically. A portion of one's existence examined carefully for meaning. As in a novel, the main character (the author) should be transformed in a way that is interesting and satisfying to readers, and he or she should arrive in a new place. My simple, romantic statement at the end of the last chapter suggests that this was successfully accomplished, that I had undergone such a magical transformation.

But memoirs can be stylized and unrealistic, depending on an author's interpretation of the times gone by. While I sought to close this book with a strong sense that I had evolved and matured, such increments seldom happen quickly, or conveniently, simply because of the transition to a new grade in school or relocation to a new place.

I have many reasons to be thankful and satisfied with my life. Success, or attainment of my goals, or whatever description one might provide of arriving at a place I am happy to be, came slowly over many years, but it came. But the two years of my life that followed my return from Spain were a painful reminder that while a foundation for change had been established during my foibles and triumphs during that time overseas, I still had a long way to go before I was actually a confident person on the road to self-fulfillment. There were conflicts, disappointments, and reluctance to step up in my own defense when I should have. New kids are seldom popular, and middle school boys can be physically aggressive and deliberately exclusive. I guess I experienced some of both. But after a few painful years in middle school, things improved dramatically for me. I did well academically, made some very good friends, and was able to play baseball for two years, though I eventually made my way to cross-country and track. Distance running seemed to fit my slight frame.

In college, in medical school, and in residency training, I continued to improve myself and advance as well as I could have hoped. I obtained a Navy scholarship to help me afford medical school, and I eventually graduated with high honors, having skipped my senior year in college to enter medical school early. I trained in three medical specialties, and passed my boards without difficulty in all three. My initial position out of training involved a split between emergency medicine and anesthesiology, but after eight years I had to commit myself entirely to the latter. Opportunities in education and academic medicine presented themselves, and I was able, with the help of trusted mentors, to achieve promotion to full professor ten years into my academic career, a rank I did not expect I would ever attain.

I served honorably in the Navy and stayed in the reserves after my scholarship obligation was fulfilled. During that time, I was twice called up to serve in wartime, supporting the Marines during the first Gulf War and the anesthesia services at Portsmouth Navy Hospital during the Iraq/Afghanistan conflict. Eventually, I was promoted to captain, from which rank I retired.

On the personal side, I married a bit later in life and raised a little girl with my wife, Jennifer. My relationship with my family, as well as my mother and sister, has given me great joy. I have had the opportunity to write professional books and many journal articles, including research papers, reviews, and textbook chapters, all of which has been gratifying to me. Though there has been little in the way of widespread recognition or commercial success, I've written two novels, and most recently this memoir, which I hope will be inspiring to those who suffer from introversion, hesitation, or lack of confidence.

I frequently think about when I should retire, and as I survey the years of my life, I cannot help but be grateful and satisfied with my position. My achievements have required enthusiasm and dedication, but when I search for the pillars and foundations of my life, the time I spent in Spain looms large. The experiences I enjoyed during that tour, with a patient and demanding father, a loving mother, my friends, and an unforgettable fifth-grade teacher, provided a stable emotional baseline for my development. It was of great value to consider my current station while writing this book, and, poring through memories from long ago, to come to a greater understanding of who I am.

People acquire some degree of wisdom with age. And in looking back at our past lives, this wisdom provides perspective. We cannot help but wonder what made us who we are, and looking at our parents provides only a partial answer, even as we mourn their passage into frailty and death. My mother was diagnosed with colon cancer a year ago, and with her many co-existing diseases, the price of a life both demanding and well-lived, she declined surgical therapy.

"I don't want to die in a nursing home," she announced to my sister and me.

She was fearful, not of death itself, but of gradual decomposition and suffering with bedsores and opportunistic infections in a foreign, unwelcome environment. I could not contradict her, for I had seen this scenario play out many times in medicine. There is reason to fear this sort of conclusion to life. Since the death of my father from cancer at fifty years of age after a year of fruitless therapy, my mother had spoken openly of dying. It was not frightening to her.

We have feared the worst, but God the Father has been extraordinarily kind to our small family, and my mother carries on almost three years into her illness, tolerating her discomforts and bearing her dysfunction as best she can. She ambles for short distances with canes or walkers, takes care of the dog, goes for rides to get ice cream, and relishes our picnics and cookouts. Every Saturday I drive to her house, where she and my sister make me lunch, often one that reminds me of our lives together when I was a boy. It has been an extraordinary time to celebrate our family, our values, and our prior lives together. After we eat, I sit with her on the couch or their small deck, and we look at old photo albums, an activity I had formerly avoided as best I could.

What, I wondered, could old photos stir within me that was meaningful? After many months, I have come full circle—the opportunity to comb through the images of relatives on both sides of my family has provided to me a sense of self and belonging that I could not have predicted. Most importantly, this endeavor has been fulfilling for my mother. Discussing her family, relatives, and friends, as well as her mistakes, triumphs, and adventures, provides a healing balm in these times of frequent physical discomfort and occasional depression. Mom lights up with verve and enthusiasm as we discuss those people who touched her life and the times in which they lived. I did not previously understand how important such a journey would be for an older person, especially one who has been gripped by a fatal disease. In addition, these explorations also satisfy elements of my own curiosity.

I will carry these reflections with me until I die myself. When I close my eyes and think about my mother's vivid descriptions, I can see the dilapidated old house she inhabited in Johnstown, just above the railroad tracks, and I can picture the soot from the mills and the railroad collecting on the linens hung out to dry, the clamor as her grandmother raced to pull the laundry in when the train passed, hissing and spewing cinders. I can feel the terror Mom experienced when her stepfather became cruel and angry, unable to cope with the behavior of four unruly children. Her reasons for leaving home at seventeen to join the Air Force, lying about her complete lack of flying experience in order to begin training as a stewardess in the newly created Military Air Transport System, are now apparent. She flushed with pride as she discussed the maneuvers on which she accompanied the flight crews for safety and emergency landings. It saddened me to learn she had been required to leave the profession to marry my father and raise a family. The U.S. military did not permit both spouses to be in the active service in those days. Instead, she became a housewife, relegated to working behind a checkout counter at a Sears and Roebuck department store instead of flying around the world in Constellations.

Mom dug deeper to acquaint me with her forebears. Her uncle by marriage had been a celebrated musician who played with Glenn Miller during and after World War II. Her grandfather had likewise been a gifted pianist who performed in Vaudeville acts and was later recognized by the president for his service to American soldiers in the European theater, supporting such luminaries as Bob Hope.

Her beloved Aunt Fannie moved to Baltimore to become a welder, one of millions of Rosie the Riveter women in World War II. She later was widowed when her Uncle Johny, my mother's favorite uncle, drowned in a swimming pool, leaving her to raise two children alone. A cousin married a famous clarinetist, a virtuoso who played with Glenn Miller during the war and subsequently a number of big bands that were conducted on radio and television by other famous conductors. And I learned more about Mom's father, a "Canadian Brit" who was deported for philandering and failing to support his family. He later remarried a Canadian woman and sired several more children. While raising her own young family, my mother went to visit him and was moved by his impoverished existence.

Most affecting of all, we saw a few photos of my own father during his last few months among us, taken when we had little idea he would soon be gone. I never effectively mourned for him, turning soon after his demise to my studies, as the second year of medical school was quite consuming. But his death had left our family in a state of shock and turmoil. My mother and sister scattered, and the place I called home for the longest period of my life was sold, leaving little trace of our presence in Boiling Springs. Surprisingly, just a decade after his demise, my sister, my mother, and I reunited in a small house we purchased together, living in relative harmony for several years in a late-life affirmation of the love we'd once held for each other, a circumstance I believe would have given my father great pride and satisfaction.

And through all these considerations and discussions of times and relations I have had with my mother, I have developed a much greater respect for what we leave behind as we perish from this earth. Twenty years ago, I would not have considered devoting my Saturday afternoons to oral recollections. Now I covet these hours. Meaningful moments of life slip away from us each day, and we provide value to them, not just by living them, but by recollecting them and assigning emotional significance in a considered manner.

The lyrics from the Genesis song "Home by the Sea," have always resonated with me, but they do so even more today, as I've acquired a greater degree of maturity and understanding with age. I hope I shall have the opportunity to sit with a younger person and discuss the meaning of my life, as my time runs out, in the decades to come. Hopefully, this memoir itself will provide some material for those discussions. I will be all the more fulfilled.

Postscript: During the final editing of this book, my mother succumbed to her illness. We were graced with several years of quality existence after her cancer was diagnosed, for which I am most grateful. As these pages reveal, she was an ardent supporter of mine, providing love, guidance and inspiration in my life. For her kindness and wisdom, I am forever indebted; I will remember her with great affection for the remainder of my days.

About the Author

Steve Orebaugh practices anesthesiology at a university medical center in western Pennsylvania. After medical school, he trained in emergency medicine, critical care, and anesthesiology, eventually settling on the latter as his long-term profession. His areas of interest and expertise are acute pain management and regional anesthesia, which is the provision of nerve blocks to help control postoperative pain. Much of his time is spent providing education for hospital residents, both didactic and clinical bedside teaching. He also performs clinical research and has had over one hundred articles and textbook chapters published in anesthesia and emergency medicine literature. He enjoys creative as well as professional writing, and has published two novels, two medical texts (one as co-author), and a patient education monograph.

As a member of an Air Force family, his early life was spent traversing the globe with his father, who was assigned to a number of interesting places. Steve has lived in many different areas, throughout the U.S. and overseas, courtesy of the Air Force, his medical training, and the Navy, which he joined to pay for medical school. The geographical, social, and cultural variety he experienced early in his life instilled in him a sense of curiosity and an interest in animals, science, and biology. Eventually, this led to his career in medicine and his desire to share what he has experienced and learned through his writing.

www.ingramcontent.com/pod-product-compliance
Lightning Source LLC
Chambersburg PA
CBHW011159090426
42740CB00020B/3410